Worship Supplement

Worship
SUPPLEMENT

Authorized by the
COMMISSION ON WORSHIP

The Lutheran Church—Missouri Synod
and
Synod of Evangelical Lutheran Churches

Concordia Publishing House
Saint Louis　　London

MANUFACTURED IN THE UNITED STATES OF AMERICA

Contents

	Page
Foreword	9
Acknowledgments	11
List of Abbreviations, Terms, and Symbols	13
Suggestions for the Worshiper	15
Liturgical Section	17
The Holy Eucharist I	19
Seasonal Offertories	30
Forms of the Intercessions	33
Another Form of the Intercessions	41
Proper Prefaces	42
Prayer of Thanksgiving	45
Post-Communion Collects	47
Rubrics for the Minister	49
A Form for Private Confession and Absolution	54
An Order for Public Confession	55
An Order for Corporate Confession and Absolution	56
The Holy Eucharist II	59
The Holy Eucharist III	63
A Morning Service	68
Seasonal Invitatory Versicles and Responses	78
The Responsive Prayer for Morning	79
An Evening Service	85
The Responsive Prayer for Evening	90
Responsories	95
A Service of Prayer and Preaching I	100
A Service of Prayer and Preaching II	103
A Service of Prayer and Preaching III	106
Sentences for the Services of Prayer and Preaching	110
The Office of Prime	112
The Noonday Office	116
The Office of Compline	118

	Hymn Numbers
The Christian Year	701 – 758
Adventtide	701 – 707
Christmastide	708 – 720
Epiphanytide	721 – 722
Transfiguration	723 – 724
Lent/Holy Week	725 – 726
Palm Sunday	727
Good Friday	728 – 730
Holy Saturday	731 – 732
Eastertide	733 – 742
Ascensiontide	743 – 744
The Trinity	745 – 755
Minor Festivals	756 – 758
The Church	759 – 783
Christian Unity	759
Mission	760 – 761
Baptism	762 – 763
Holy Communion	764 – 766
Prayer	767
Worship and Praise	768 – 773
Anniversary	774
Social Concern	775 – 779
Marriage	780
Youth	781
Family and Home	782
Trust	783
The Nation	784 – 787
Peace	785 – 787
Times and Seasons	788 – 793
Morning	788 – 789
Evening	790
New Year	791
Thanksgiving	792 – 793
	Page
Indexes	231

Foreword

More than a generation has passed since *The Lutheran Hymnal* first appeared in 1941. The intervening years have brought many changes in Christian living that have led to new worship needs. New concerns for social structures, colleges, armed forces, missions, the inner city, and racially or culturally conscious groups have raised a need for updating liturgical and hymnodic materials both as to language and form.

When this need first began to be felt, a thorough revision of *The Lutheran Hymnal* was planned and begun. The project was abandoned several years ago in favor of a program designed to lead to an eventual all-Lutheran hymnal in English. The present *Worship Supplement* was meanwhile chosen to supply the worship needs of the Church until the proposed long-range project could produce a more permanent hymnal. It was adopted as a convenient stage in the development of new types and forms of worship materials which, by meeting the demands of changing times and situations, might serve also as a modern experiment in applying timeless truths to timely needs, an attempt to give voice to the cries and joys of today's Christian by means of contemporary creations.

Much of the language of the liturgies and the hymns was found to be in need of revision to make it meaningful to the man of today. In some liturgical texts the Commission on Worship produced its own revised versions (Gloria, Te Deum), in others it adopted those suggested by the Committee on Common Liturgical Texts (Our Father, Apostolic Creed, Nicene Creed).

The Commission was also interested in restoring appropriate materials that had fallen into disuse and in preparing or adapting new materials for today. Additional revised offertories, prayers, collects, and other historic forms are provided. Several new services are included. Among the latter are two orders for Holy Communion designed for special use and three experimental services of prayer and preaching. Other new items include the Old Testament Lesson, an expanded Kyrie, the singing of the Offertory as the offerings are brought forward, congregational responses and petitions in the Intercessions, and the Prayer of Thanksgiving.

The Commission wishes to supply examples of traditional hymns revised for modern use and new hymns relevant to the life of the Christian in the world today.

Worship Supplement is issued in two books: one, a tune-text edition for the orders of service and the hymns; the other, a keyboard edition containing the accompaniments. All melodies have been set in a comfortable singing range. The most convenient notation, generally the quarter note, has been used. Bar lines are used when they help and are suppressed when they hinder the understanding of the rhythmic layout of the tune.

The melodies for the orders of service are entirely new; no historic compositions, fragments of the same, or chants have been retained. These tunes move about in a comfortable middle range. In the short responses no meters are indicated, and only short and long notes (quarters and halves) are used; their precise time values are derived from the text.

The longer compositions (for example, "Lord, Have Mercy," "Holy, Holy, Holy," and "Lamb of God") are nonmetrical yet rhythmic, for they seek to present the text as naturally as possible. But in each composition the generative musical material has been held to a minimum to facilitate learning and to promote unity. The music of the liturgy is the work of Paul Bunjes and Richard Hillert, both members of the Music Committee of the Commission on Worship.

For the 93 hymn texts, 87 tunes were assembled (six tunes serve two hymns each), of which 10 are original melodies introduced into a service book for the first time. Sources of texts and tunes are given with the individual hymns. The numbering of the hymns begins at 701 for convenient reference.

It is the hope of the Commission that the worship materials presented in this booklet may be a God-pleasing addition to existing hymnals, serve the present needs of the Church, and be a helpful contribution to service books of the future. Throughout its work of expanding the Church's worship resources, the Commission made every effort to preserve the Church's dedication to true worship and Biblical doctrine.

"Something must be dared in the name of Christ." — Martin Luther (first order of service, 1523).

COMMISSION ON WORSHIP

Acknowledgments

The Commission on Worship herewith expresses its gratitude to the persons and institutions named below for their permission to include in the *Worship Supplement* the copyright items listed.

Beacon Press, Boston, Mass., for the text of "The Voice of God Is Calling" (776), from *The Collected Hymns of John Haynes Holmes,* copyright 1960.

Christianity Today, Washington, D. C., for the text of "The Sending, Lord, Springs from Thy Yearning Heart" (761), copyright 1966.

The Church Pension Fund, New York, for the texts of "Our Father, by Whose Name" (782) and "That Easter Day with Joy Was Bright" (737), from *The Hymnal 1940.*

Commission on the Liturgy and Hymnal for the text of "Deep Were His Wounds and Red" (726) and its tune *Marlee,* from *Service Book and Hymnal,* No. 80.

Commission on Worship and Spiritual Life, Lutheran World Federation, Geneva, Switzerland, for the English texts of "Grant Peace, We Pray, in Mercy, Lord" (785) and "Lord God, Thy Praise We Sing" (745), from *Laudamus.*

The Community of the Resurrection, Mirfield, Yorkshire, England, for the text of "Holy Spirit, Ever Dwelling" (754).

Gwenlyn Evans, Ltd., Caernarvon, Wales, United Kingdom, for the tune *Ebenezer* (747).

Carl Fischer, Inc., New York, and Gordon V. Thompson, Ltd., Toronto, Canada, for the text of "Gentle Mary Laid Her Child" (716).

Dr. Harry Emerson Fosdick, Bronxville, New York, for the text of "God of Grace and God of Glory" (778).

The H. W. Gray Co., Inc., New York, for the tune *The King's Majesty* (727), copyright 1941.

The Proprietors of *Hymns Ancient and Modern,* Worthing, Sussex, England, for the text of "Good Christian Men, Rejoice and Sing" (736).

The Hymn Society of America, New York, for the texts of "Hope of the World" (749), from *Eleven Ecumenical Hymns,* copyright 1954, and "Forgive Us, Lord, for Shallow Thankfulness" (792), from *My God Is There, Controlling,* copyright 1965.

A List of Abbreviations, Terms, and Symbols

abr. — abridged

alt. — altered

ascr. — ascribed to

c. — circa, about

cento — a hymn consisting of selected stanzas of a longer original

CM — common meter (4 lines: 8.6.8.6 syllables)

composite — the work of more than one author or translator

D — double

d. — died

LM — long meter (4 lines: 8.8.8.8 syllables)

paraphr. — paraphrased by

R. — response, sung or spoken by the congregation

SM — short meter (4 lines: 6. 6. 8. 6 syllables)

st., sts. — stanza(s)

trans. — translated by, translator

V. — versicle, sung or spoken by the minister or leader

ᶤ — the congregation stands

꜔ — the congregation is seated

.ꜱ — the congregation kneels

✠ — the sign of the cross is made

† — slightly altered

★ — the stanza may be omitted if the hymn is to be shortened

A List of Abbreviations, Terms, and Symbols

SUGGESTIONS FOR THE WORSHIPER

Come to church early enough to spend some moments in preparatory prayer and meditation.

Before taking your place, pause and bow toward the cross as a sign of your reverence for God.

Having come to your place, bow your head or kneel, make the sign of the cross as a reminder of your baptism, and say a prayer for reverent participation in worship. You may include an examination of conscience and a silent confession of sin.

If there is time, read through the propers for the day, or pray a psalm or a few collects.

In general, before the service begins, spend the time in focusing your mind on God your Maker, on the redemptive work of your Lord Jesus Christ, and wait upon the coming of the Holy Spirit through Word and Sacrament.

THE SERVICE

Note carefully the directions as to when to stand, sit, or kneel. Knowing what posture to assume is part of your worship; it should not be necessary for the pastor to indicate to you what to do.

Note also whatever variations are likely to occur in the liturgy for the day. Being prepared for these as they occur, and knowing the reason for them, is also a responsibility of true worship.

To follow the texts of the propers for the day, turn to the page in the Hymnal where these are to be found, and keep the page available for ready reference and participation as the service proceeds.

Think of yourself as a priest of God, functioning as such in the great priesthood of all believers, rejoicing in the privileges of your baptism, and bringing an offering of praise and thanksgiving through Jesus Christ and in the Holy Spirit.

CUSTOMS AND PRACTICES

The *sign of the cross* is made by touching the tips of the fingers to the forehead, the breast, and then both shoulders in turn. This is appropriately done at the Trinitarian Invocation, at the last phrase of the Creed, before and after receiving the elements of Holy Communion, and at the Benediction.

Bowing is proper on entering church, during the first half of the Gloria Patri, on approaching the altar for Holy Communion, and on leaving the pew after the conclusion of the service. Bowing more deeply, or kneeling, is customary at the words of the Nicene Creed "he was born . . . and became Man." Bowing only the head is appropriate at any mention of the sacred name of Jesus, especially where this occurs in the Creed.

RECEIVING HOLY COMMUNION

It is good practice to kneel in prayer, or to bow while seated, before approaching the altar to receive the Sacrament.

If the ceremony of the Greeting of Peace (Pax) is practiced, this is done immediately after the Pax in the following manner. Each worshiper extends both his hands to clasp the right hand of his neighbor, beginning with those nearest the center aisle and progressing to the side aisles. As he does so, he says, "Peace be with you," and the neighbor may respond with the same words. Then the neighbor turns to the next person, and the same things are said and done until all have participated in this sign of fellowship in Christ.

Immediately before receiving the body of Christ, each communicant may say silently, "Lord, I am not worthy to have you come under my roof, but only say the word, and your servant will be healed"; before receiving the blood of Christ, he may say silently: "What shall I render to the Lord for all his bounty to me? I will lift up the cup of salvation and call on the name of the Lord." He may also silently say "Amen" when the minister says, "The body of Christ," and again on hearing the words "The blood of Christ."

Upon returning to his place, each communicant should kneel, or bow while seated, and speak a prayer of thanksgiving.

16

Liturgical Section

The Holy Eucharist
I

THE SERVICE OF THE WORD

The Entrance Song
(INTROIT)

(Texts on pages 54 – 94 in The Lutheran Hymnal)

Lord, Have Mercy
(KYRIE)

℣. In peace let us pray to the Lord.

℟. A - men.

℣. For the peace that is from a - bove and for the salvation

of our souls let us pray to the Lord.

℟. Lord,___ have mer - cy.
Ky -ri - e e - lei - son.

℣. For the peace of the whole — world, for the well-being of the church - es of God, and for the u - ni - ty of all let us pray to the Lord.

℞. Christ,— have mer - cy.
Chri - ste e - lei - son.

℣. For this ho - ly house and for those who in faith, pi - e - ty, and fear of God offer here their wor - ship and praise let us pray to the Lord.

℞ Lord, —— have mer - cy.
Ky - ri - e e - lei - son.

℣. Help,— save,— pity and de-fend us, O God, by your grace.

℞ A - men.

Or

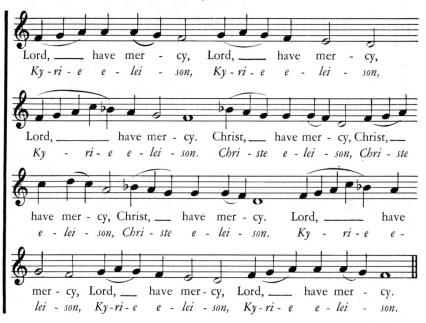

Lord, ____ have mer - cy, Lord, ____ have mer - cy,
Ky - ri - e   e - lei - son,   Ky - ri - e   e - lei - son,

Lord, _____ have mer - cy.   Christ, ___ have mer - cy, Christ, ___
Ky - ri - e   e - lei - son.   Chri - ste   e - lei - son, Chri - ste

have mer - cy, Christ, ___ have mer - cy.   Lord, _____ have
e - lei - son, Chri - ste   e - lei - son.   Ky - ri - e   e -

mer - cy, Lord, ___ have mer - cy, Lord, ___ have mer - cy.
lei - son, Ky - ri - e   e - lei - son, Ky - ri - e   e - lei - son.

Or

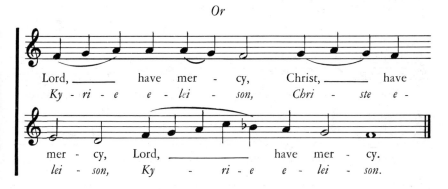

Lord, _____ have mer - cy,   Christ, _____ have
Ky - ri - e   e - lei - son,   Chri - ste   e -

mer - cy, Lord, _____ have mer - cy.
lei - son, Ky - ri - e   e - lei - son.

Glory and Praise
(GLORIA IN EXCELSIS)

Glory and Praise *is omitted during Advent and from Ash Wednesday through Holy Saturday. It may be omitted generally except in festival seasons. It may be sung antiphonally, as indicated.*

All

Glo - ry   be   to   God   on   high! And   on   earth peace through God's

21

good will to men. We praise you, we bless you, we worship you, we glorify you. We give thanks to you for your great glory. Lord God, heavenly King, God Father Almighty. Lord Jesus Christ, only-begotten Son, Lord God, Lamb of God, Son of the Father. You take away the sin of the world. You are seated at the right hand of the Father; have mercy on us and receive our prayer. You alone are the Holy One. You alone are the Lord. You alone are the Most High, Jesus Christ, with the Holy Spirit, in the glory of God the Father. Amen.

The Salutation

℣. The Lord be with you.

R̹. And with your spir - it.

The Collect

(Texts on pages 54—94 in The Lutheran Hymnal)

R̹. A - men.

The Lesson

The Gradual

(Texts on pages 54—94 in The Lutheran Hymnal)

*From the First Sunday After Easter through Pentecost
the following Paschal Verse shall be sung in place of the Gradual:*

℣. The Lord is ris - en!

R̹. The Lord is ris - en! He is ris - en in - deed!

The Epistle

The Alleluia and Sentence or the Tract
(Texts on pages 54—94 in The Lutheran Hymnal)

The Holy Gospel

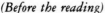

(Before the reading)

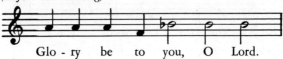

Glo - ry   be   to   you,   O   Lord.

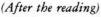

(After the reading)

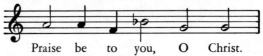

Praise   be   to   you,   O   Christ.

A Hymn may be sung.

The Sermon

The Creed

The Creed may be omitted at weekday services.

We believe in one God, the Father, the Almighty,
    Maker of heaven and earth,
    of all things visible and invisible.

We believe in the one Lord, Jesus Christ,
    the only-begotten Son of God,
    Son of the Father from all eternity:
    God from God, Light from Light, true God from true God:
    begotten, not made, one in being with the Father.
    Through him all things were made.
    For us men and for our salvation he came from heaven;
        by the power of the Holy Spirit
        he was born of the Virgin Mary, and became Man.
    For our sake he was crucified under Pontius Pilate;
        he suffered, died, and was buried.
    He arose on the third day
        in fulfillment of the Scriptures.
    He entered into heaven and is seated
        at the right hand of the Father.
    He will come again in glory to judge the living
        and the dead,
    and his kingdom will have no end.

We believe in the Holy Spirit, the Lord,
    the Giver of life;
he proceeds from the Father and the Son.
Together with the Father and the Son
    he is worshiped and glorified.
He has spoken through the prophets.
We believe in one, holy, catholic, and apostolic Church.
We acknowledge one baptism for the forgiveness of sins.
We look for the resurrection of the dead
    and the life of the world to come. Amen.

The Hymn of the Week or another Hymn shall be sung.

THE SERVICE OF THE SACRAMENT

The Offering and the Offertory

(Seasonal Offertories on pages 30 — 33)

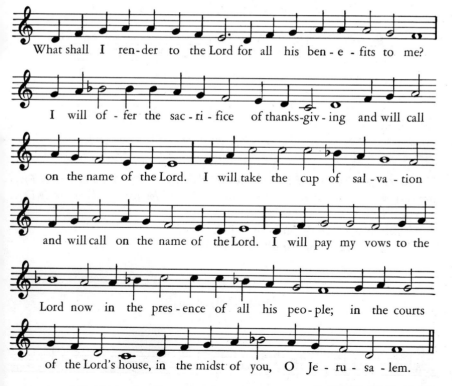

What shall I render to the Lord for all his benefits to me? I will offer the sacrifice of thanksgiving and will call on the name of the Lord. I will take the cup of salvation and will call on the name of the Lord. I will pay my vows to the Lord now in the presence of all his people; in the courts of the Lord's house, in the midst of you, O Jerusalem.

(Ps. 116:12, 17, 13, 14, 19)

25

The Intercessions

(Texts on pages 33—42)

The Preface

℣. The Lord be with you.

℟. And with your spir-it.

℣. Lift up your hearts.

℟. We lift them up to the Lord.

℣. Let us give thanks to the Lord our God.

℟. It is right and prop-er so to do.

The proper portions of the Preface are found on pages 42—45. The Proper Preface may be either seasonal or one specially appointed for the Sunday or Holy Day.

Celebrant: It is our duty and our delight . . .
evermore praising you and saying:

Holy, Holy, Holy
(SANCTUS)

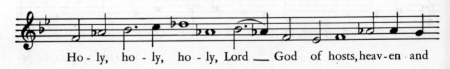

Ho-ly, ho-ly, ho-ly, Lord God of hosts, heav-en and

earth are full of your glo - ry. Ho - san - na, ho - san - na, ho - san - na in the high - est. Bless - ed is he who comes in the name of the Lord. Ho - san - na in the high - est.

The Prayer of Thanksgiving

(Texts on pages 45 − 47)

The Our Father

Our Father in heaven:
    Holy be your name,
    Your kingdom come,
    Your will be done
        on earth as in heaven.
    Give us today our daily bread.
    Forgive us our sins,
        as we forgive those who sin against us.
    Save us in the time of trial,
        and deliver us from evil,
For yours is the kingdom, the power,
and the glory forever. Amen.

The Greeting of Peace
(PAX)

℣. The peace of the Lord be with you al - way.

℟. And with your_ spir - it.

Lamb of God
(AGNUS DEI)

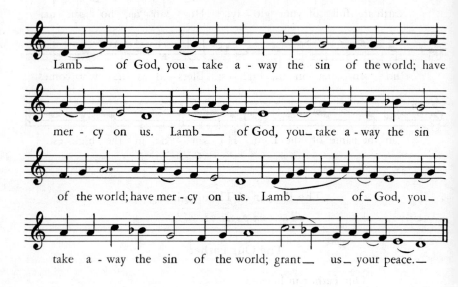

Lamb of God, you take a-way the sin of the world; have mer-cy on us. Lamb of God, you take a-way the sin of the world; have mer-cy on us. Lamb of God, you take a-way the sin of the world; grant us your peace.

The Distribution

The Thanksgiving

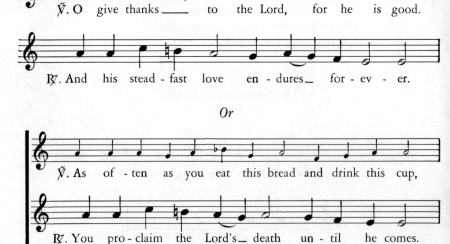

℣. O give thanks to the Lord, for he is good.

℟. And his stead-fast love en-dures for-ev-er.

Or

℣. As of-ten as you eat this bread and drink this cup,

℟. You pro-claim the Lord's death un-til he comes.

The Collect

(Texts of Post-Communion Collects on pages 47 — 49)

℟. A - men.

℣. The Lord be with you.

℟. And with your spir - it.

℣. Let us bless the Lord.

℟. Thanks be to God.

The Benediction

The Lord bless you and keep you. The Lord make his face shine up - on you and be gra - cious to you. The Lord lift up his coun - te - nance up - on you and give you ✠ peace.

Or

The bless-ing of al- might - y God the Fa-ther, the✠Son, and
the Ho - ly Spir - it be up - on you and be with_you all.

℟. A - men. A - men. A - men.

SEASONAL OFFERTORIES

Adventtide

Our God comes, he does not keep silence, before him is a devouring fire, round about him a mighty tempest.
He calls to the heavens above and to the earth, that he may judge his people:
"Gather to me my faithful ones, who made a covenant with me by sacrifice!"
Offer to God a sacrifice of thanksgiving, and pay your vows to the Most High.

(Ps. 50:3, 4, 5, 14)

Christmastide

Thanks be to God for his inexpressible gift!
Ascribe to the Lord, O families of the peoples,
ascribe to the Lord glory and strength!
Ascribe to the Lord the glory due his name;
bring an offering, and come into his courts!
Worship the Lord in holy array; tremble before him, all the earth!

(2 Cor. 9:15; Ps. 96:7-9)

Epiphanytide

Rejoice, O Gentiles, with his people, and let all the peoples praise him.
Long may he live, may gold of Sheba be given to him!

May his name endure forever, his fame continue as long
   as the sun!
May men bless themselves by him, all nations
   call him blessed!
By the mercies of God present your bodies as a living sacrifice,
   holy and acceptable to God, which is your spiritual worship.

(Rom. 15:10, 11b; Ps. 72:15, 17; Rom. 12:1b)

Lent

Be imitators of God, as beloved children. And walk in love,
   as Christ loved us and gave himself up for us, a fragrant
   offering and sacrifice to God.
Always and for everything give thanks in the name of our Lord
   Jesus Christ to God the Father.
I will give thanks to you, O Lord, among the peoples;
   I will sing praises to you among the nations.
With a free-will offering I will sacrifice to you;
   I will give thanks to your name, O Lord, for it is good.

(Eph. 5:1, 2, 20; Ps. 57:9; 54:6)

Passiontide

I will go to the altar of God, to God my exceeding joy.
The sacrifice acceptable to God is a broken spirit;
   a broken and contrite heart, O God, you will not despise.
Do good to Zion in your good pleasure; rebuild the walls of Jerusalem,
Then will you delight in right sacrifices.

(Ps. 43:4; 51:17, 18, 19a)

Eastertide

I thank you that you have answered me
   and have become my salvation.
I shall not die, but I shall live
   and recount the deeds of the Lord.
The stone which the builders rejected
   has become the chief cornerstone.
Come to him, to that living stone, and like living stones be
   yourselves built into a spiritual house, to be a holy priesthood,
   to offer spiritual sacrifices acceptable to God through Jesus Christ.

(Ps. 118:21, 17, 22; 1 Peter 2:4a, 5)

Ascensiontide

Sing praises to God, sing praises!
   Sing praises to our King, sing praises!

31

For the shields of the earth belong to God;
    he is highly exalted!
Hark, glad songs of victory in the tents of the righteous:
    "The right hand of the Lord does valiantly,
    the right hand of the Lord is exalted,
    the right hand of the Lord does valiantly!"
Open to me the gates of righteousness,
    that I may enter through them and give thanks to the Lord.

(Ps. 47:6, 10; 118:15, 16, 19)

Whitsuntide

With mighty chariotry, twice ten thousand,
    thousands upon thousands,
    the Lord came from Sinai into the holy place.
When he ascended on high, he led a host of captives,
    and he gave gifts to men.
Summon your might, O God;
    show your strength, O God, for you have wrought for us.
Because of your temple at Jerusalem kings bear gifts to you.
My vows to you I must perform, O God;
    I will render thank offerings to you.
For you have delivered my soul from death,
    yes, my feet from falling,
    that I may walk before God in the light of life.

(Ps. 68:17; Eph. 4:8; Ps. 68:28-29; 56:12-13)

After Pentecost

My eyes have seen the King, the Lord of hosts!
And I heard the voice of the Lord saying, "Whom shall I send,
    and who will go for us?"
Then I said, "Here I am! Send me."
And he said, "Go."
Teach me the way I should go,
    for to you I lift up my soul.
Teach me to do your will,
    for you are my God!
My mouth will speak the praise of the Lord,
    and let all flesh bless his holy name forever and ever.

(Is. 6:5b, 8, 9a; Ps. 143:8b, 10; 145:21)

There is one God, the Father, from whom are all things
    and for whom we exist,

32

And one Lord, Jesus Christ, through whom are all things
   and through whom we exist.
Do you not know that your body is a temple of the Holy Spirit within
   you, which you have from God?
You are not your own; you were bought with a price.
   So glorify God in your body.
I will give thanks to you, O Lord, my God, with my whole heart,
   and I will glorify your name forever.

(1 Cor. 8:6; 6:19-20; Ps. 86:12)

By a single offering he has perfected for all time those who
   are sanctified.
Therefore, brethren, since we have confidence to enter the sanctuary
   by the blood of Jesus, by the new and living way,
Let us draw near with a true heart in full assurance of faith;
Let us hold fast the confession of our hope without wavering,
   for he who promised is faithful;
And let us consider how to stir up one another to love and good works,
   not neglecting to meet together, as is the habit of some,
   but encouraging one another,
And all the more as you see the Day drawing near.
Therefore let us be grateful for receiving a kingdom that cannot
   be shaken,
And thus let us offer to God acceptable worship, with reverence
   and awe;
For our God is a consuming fire.

(Heb. 10:14, 19-20a, 22a, 23-25; 12:28-29)

FORMS OF THE INTERCESSIONS

At the time of the Intercessions in the Eucharist, prayer may be made according to the pattern here following. After each "let us pray" the congregation should make some response, such as, "Kyrie, eleison," or "Lord, hear our prayer," or "We ask you to hear us, good Lord." Some items may be omitted, and others may be added, at the discretion of the minister. An alternate pattern calls for an assistant minister, or a layman, to bid the congregation to prayer, saying, "Let us pray for . . . ," after which the celebrant should read an appropriate Collect, the congregation responding, as always, "Amen." It is always proper to pray for particular persons by name.

Adventtide

We rejoice, not only in Christ's presence among us but in the knowledge that this saving presence will be one day fully manifest in glory. Let us pray for ourselves and for all of God's people, that this our hope incite us to greater faith and love:

For the Church, promise of mankind's long-awaited unity and peace,
For all public servants, that they zealously promote justice and the common good,
For the younger nations of the world, that as brothers we assist them in their progress toward a fuller life, let us pray:

R. Lord, have mercy.

For businessmen and salesmen, that this world's commerce reflect the brotherhood of heaven,
For the hungry and the homeless, and for all men deprived of their heritage as God's children,
For the aged and the infirm, that we cherish Christ in them and surround them with our care,
For those who may meet with sudden death, that they find peace in God's merciful judgment, let us pray:

R. Lord, hear our prayer.

For a truly apostolic parish community, intent on an authentic Christian presence in society,
For the renewal of our parish worship, source of all spiritual vitality and fulfillment,
For this holy assembly, that the Eucharist be for us the pledge of eternal glory, let us pray:

R. We ask you to hear us, good Lord.

Be merciful, Lord God, listen to the prayers of your Church; grant us, through the blessed coming of your Son, the help of your grace in this present life and eternal happiness as our reward in heaven; through Jesus Christ, your Son, our Lord. Amen.

Christmastide

The Word became flesh in order that all men might be revealed as God's sons. Let us pray for our own parish community, for the Church throughout the world, and for all men, that we may respond wholeheartedly to the appeal of God's love:

For the Church, visible sign of Christ's saving presence among men,
For all the clergy, that their lives echo the holy Word they preach,

For all who still walk in darkness, that they come to know Christ, the Light of the world, let us pray:

R. Lord, have mercy.

For statesmen and world leaders, that they strive earnestly for peace and unity among nations,

For the new year we begin, that it mark a new dedication to the cause of peace and human liberty,

For artists, architects, and craftsmen, that their work mirror the truth and integrity of creation, let us pray:

R. Lord, hear our prayer.

For members of the armed services, and for all men and women stationed far from home,

For orphans and children of broken homes, that they find love and affection and a sense of belonging,

For those who die alone and forgotten, that they rejoice forever in the company of the saints, let us pray:

R. We ask you to hear us, good Lord.

For the charitable organizations of our parish, and for all of our efforts for the relief of the poor,

For liturgical renewal in our parish, that we may better manifest the mystery of Christ in his Church,

For this holy assembly, that nourished with the eucharistic bread and wine, we may bear Christ in our lives, let us pray:

R. Mercifully hear the prayers of your people, Lord God, as we rejoice in the mystery of the Incarnation; grant that the divine light with which you flood our minds may shine forth in our lives; through Jesus Christ, your Son, our Lord. Amen.

Lent

Now is the favorable time, now is the day of salvation. Let us pray for ourselves and for the Church throughout the world, that God restore us, through true repentance, to the holiness to which we have been called in Christ Jesus:

For the Church, God's people continually summoned to renew the covenant,

For all ministers of the Word, ordained for the healing of Christ in his members,

For the Church's catechetical work, for all our brothers and sisters charged with leading men to Christ, let us pray:

R. Lord, have mercy.

For understanding among nations, and for a feasible plan for general disarmament in our time,

For housewives and all homemakers, that their devotion inspire us to all forms of Christian service,

For social workers, that they comfort the disinherited and give them a new sense of their dignity, let us pray:

R. Lord, hear our prayer.

For prisoners and exiles, for orphans, and for all the world's lonely and depressed,

For all the physically and mentally ill, that we see Christ in them and surround them with our care, let us pray:

R. We ask you to hear us, good Lord.

For our catechumens, that God grant them faith and repentance and bring them to the waters of rebirth,

For those estranged from the Church's sacramental life, that we may soon rejoice in full communion with them,

For this holy assembly, that the Eucharist may have its full effect of charity in our lives, let us pray:

R. Hear our prayers, Lord God, and look mercifully upon our penance; grant that your Church, cleansed of sin, may approach Easter with spiritual joy; through Jesus Christ, your Son, our Lord. Amen.

Eastertide

Christ, raised from the dead, will never die again; death has no more power over him. Let us pray for ourselves and for all Christ's members, that as we have been baptized into his saving death, so we may proclaim his resurrection to all men:

For the Church, witness to the risen Christ, mankind's victory over sin and death,

For all preachers of the Gospel, that they may proclaim the promise of a new heaven and a new earth,

For all the newly baptized, that the Spirit bring them to a full knowledge of Christ's love, let us pray:

R. Lord, have mercy.

For the United Nations, and for all agencies dedicated to the cause of international peace and cooperation,

For economic and social progress, for the prospect of a fully human life for all men,

For continuing scientific research, that we may exploit our wonderful inheritance as God's children, let us pray:

R. Lord, hear our prayer.

For favorable weather, that we may praise God for the earth's renewed fertility,

For all of suffering humanity, that God grant us the means of embracing them with our charity, let us pray:

R. We ask you to hear us, good Lord.

For those to be confirmed, that in the power of the Spirit they may witness to the fullness of God's love,

For all our parish organizations, that they dedicate themselves to the Church's program for renewal,

For this holy assembly, that our communion in the body of the risen Christ prepare us for a share in his glory, let us pray:

R. Lord God, mercifully hear the prayers of your Church, as we rejoice in the mystery of the Resurrection; grant that what we celebrate with faith we may put into practice in our lives; through Jesus Christ, your Son, our Lord. Amen.

Whitsuntide

God's love has flooded our hearts through the gift of his Holy Spirit. Let us pray for ourselves and for the Church everywhere, that we may persevere in grace, and for all men, that we may share with them the joy we have in the unity of Christ:

For the Church, fellowship of the Spirit sent into men's hearts crying "Abba, Father,"

For all who have been commissioned by the Church to work in foreign lands, that the Holy Spirit confirm them in their apostolic mission,

For those engaged in lay witnessing, Christ's own ministry for the consecration of the world, let us pray:

R. Lord, have mercy.

For all public servants, that they may fulfill their mandate with wisdom and prudence,

For students, teachers, and scholars, that their dedication to the truth inspire us all to greater fulfillment,

For writers, editors, and publishers, that they champion the cause of truth with courage and wisdom, let us pray:

R. Lord, hear our prayer.

For the homeless and the hungry, and for all men deprived of their heritage as God's children,

For the physically and mentally ill, that our charity provide them with an experience of God's abiding love, let us pray:

R. We ask you to hear us, good Lord.

For all the parents of our parish, that God teach them how to foster the gifts of the Spirit in their children,

For adult parishioners in the single state, that they find fulfillment in the service of their fellowmen,

For this holy assembly, that sealed with the promised Spirit, we may witness to the fullness of God's love, let us pray:

R. Be merciful, Lord God, and hear our prayers; may your Holy Spirit, who is himself pleading for us, guide your Church into all truth and holiness; through Jesus Christ, your Son, our Lord. Amen.

Throughout the Year I

✝ Now that we have heard God's holy Word, let us pray for our parish community and for the Church everywhere, that we may be faithful witnesses before all men to his saving love:

For the Church, standard raised among the nations for the gathering of God's people,

For the clergy of the Church, that the Holy Spirit confirm them in their apostolic mission,

For all Christians, that beyond our divisions we seek the unity to which we are called, let us pray:

R. Lord, have mercy.

For all public servants, that they zealously promote justice and the common good,

For industrial workers, that their productivity prove a blessing for all classes of society,

For favorable weather, that we may give thanks for a good harvest, let us pray:

R. Lord, hear our prayer.

For the unemployed, and for all victims of social injustice and discrimination,

For the hungry and the homeless, and for all men deprived of their heritage as God's children, let us pray:

R. We ask you to hear us, good Lord.

For the young men and women of our parish, that Christian idealism inspire them in the choice of a profession,

For the renewal of our parish worship, source of all spiritual vitality and fulfillment,

For this holy assembly, that the life-giving bread we break and the cup we bless nurture us to the full stature of Christ, let us pray:

R. God, our Refuge and Strength, listen to the devout prayers of your Church, for you yourself have inspired them; grant that what we ask for with faith we may obtain without fail; through Jesus Christ, your Son, our Lord. Amen.

Throughout the Year II

It is the will of God our Savior that all men find salvation and come to know the truth. Let us pray for our own parish community and for all of God's people, that persevering in grace, we may proclaim the kingdom of heaven in our lives:

For the Church, Jerusalem on high, our mother, in labor until Christ is fully formed in us,

For our pastors, that they may be faithful stewards of God's mysteries,

For missionaries at home and abroad, that they preach the message of salvation in the Spirit, with much power, let us pray:

R. Lord, have mercy.

For statesmen and world leaders, that they strive earnestly for peace and unity among nations,

For farmers and ranchers, that the good earth yield to their labors for the welfare of all mankind,

For service workers of all kinds, that we welcome our dependence on them as a sign of brotherhood, let us pray:

R. Lord, hear our prayer.

For the aged and the infirm, that we cherish Christ in them and surround them with our care,

(For the victims of the _____ in _____, and) for all stricken by sudden and unexpected disaster,

For those who die alone and forgotten, that they rejoice forever in the company of the saints, let us pray:

R. We ask you to hear us, good Lord.

For the families of our parish, schools of the Lord's service for the upbuilding of his Church,

For our parish mission, that with generous hearts we respond to the grace of renewal,

For this holy assembly, that we may present ourselves as a living sacrifice, holy and acceptable to God, let us pray:

R. Your infinite kindness, almighty God, exceeds not only our merits but our prayers as well; pour out your mercy upon us, forgiving our sins, and grant us even more than we presume to ask for; through Jesus Christ, your Son, our Lord. Amen.

Throughout the Year III

In response to the holy Word proclaimed, let us pray for ourselves, that we may be faithful, and for all men, that they may find in the Church the one hope of God's call:

For the Church, built up with living stones into a temple for God in the Spirit,

For our pastors and for their ministry of praise and sanctification,

For vocations to the ministry, that Christ in his members may continue to serve the Father, let us pray:

R. Lord, have mercy.

For our civic leaders, that they guide us in the pursuit of racial equality and social justice,

For all professional people, that they challenge us with the vision of a more humane world,

(For the elections next _____, that all our decisions may be for the common good,) let us pray:

R. Lord, hear our prayer.

For persecuted Christians, and for all the persecuted, that they take courage in the promise of Christ,

For the fatally ill, that God grant them the grace of persevering in his love,

For those who may meet with sudden death, that they find peace in God's merciful judgment, let us pray:

R. We ask you to hear us, good Lord.

For our parish school, that both teachers and students advance in wisdom and grace,

For those to be confirmed, that in the power of the Spirit they may witness to the fullness of God's love,

For this holy assembly, that our communion in one bread and one cup unite us in one body for the service of one Lord, let us pray:

R. Lord God, source of all that is good, mercifully hear the prayers of your people; grant that we may advance without faltering towards the fulfillment of your promises; through Jesus Christ, your Son, our Lord. Amen.

ANOTHER FORM OF THE INTERCESSIONS

Most high and holy God, we humbly ask you to accept these your own gifts which we offer to your divine goodness, together with this, the sacrifice of our thanksgiving and the incense of our prayers. And here we would present and yield ourselves to you, asking you to make us true members incorporate in the mystical body of your Son, Jesus Christ, so that, in communion with your whole Church, we may make a pure offering to your name. O Lord, hear our prayer,

R. And let our cry come unto you.

Hear our prayer, O Lord, for the universal Church, that you will confirm it in the truth of your holy faith, inspire it with unity and concord, and extend and prosper it throughout the world. We pray you for those who are ordained to be ministers in your Church, that by their life and doctrine they may set forth your true and living Word and rightly administer your holy Sacraments. Especially do we call upon you for those who labor for you in the younger churches, that they may be strong and steadfast, abounding in your work. O Lord, hear our prayer,

R. And let our cry come unto you.

Bless, we pray you, our schools, hospitals, homes for the aged, and all our institutions. Bless those who minister to human need, whether of body, mind, or spirit, and grant them wisdom, strength, and love for you and their fellowmen. Let your blessing rest upon the seedtime and harvest, the commerce and industry, the leisure and rest, and the arts and culture of our people. Take under your special protection those whose toil is difficult or dangerous, and be with all who lay their hands to any useful task. Give to all men the mind of Christ and dispose our days in righteousness. Take from us all hatred and prejudice, and whatever may hinder justice and love among the races of men. O Lord, hear our prayer,

 R. And let our cry come unto you.

Remember the nations of the world, and let concord and peace prevail among them. Remember those who rule over us, and guide those who influence our lives through radio, press, and television. Remember our children, our youth, the married couples and those about to be married, the widows and orphans, and all those who are lonely, forsaken, and despairing. Remember the sick, the suffering, the persecuted, and the dying, especially those whom we name in our hearts before you. . . . Send them help from the sanctuary and strengthen them out of Zion. O Lord, hear our prayer,

 R. And let our cry come unto you.

We commemorate before you . . . (and) your blessed apostles and martyrs and all the saints who have gone before us with the sign of faith and are at peace; we praise you for the mercy and blessings shown them in their lifetime and pray you to grant us sinners a place in their fellowship and eternal life in your kingdom. O Lord, hear our prayer,

 R. And let our cry come unto you.

Finally, O Lord, we pray for ourselves and for all who confess the name of Christ, that we may show forth the praises of him who has called us out of darkness into his marvelous light. Grant that we, who do now celebrate this feast of love, may at the last be clothed with the white robes of those who shall join in the marriage supper of the Lamb. O Lord, hear our prayer,

 R. And let our cry come unto you. Amen.

THE PROPER PREFACE

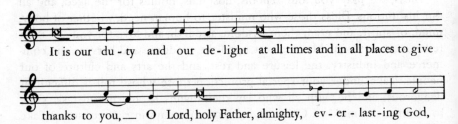

It is our du-ty and our de-light at all times and in all places to give thanks to you,— O Lord, holy Father, almighty, ev-er-last-ing God,

Adventtide

who did comfort your people with the promise of the Redeemer, through whom you will also make all things new in the day when he shall come again to judge the world in righteousness;

Christmas and until the twelfth day thereafter

through Jesus Christ, our Lord; for in the mystery of the Word made flesh you have given us a new revelation of your glory, that, seeing you in the Person of your Son, we may be drawn to the love of those things which are not seen;

Epiphanytide

through Jesus Christ, our Lord; and now do we praise you that you did send to us your only-begotten Son, and that in him, being found in human form, you did manifest the fullness of your glory;

Lent up to the Saturday before Passion Sunday, but not during the weeks from Septuagesima to Ash Wednesday

through Jesus Christ, our Lord, who was in every respect tempted as we are, yet without sinning; by whose grace we are enabled to subdue all sinful desires, and live no longer for ourselves but for him who died for us and rose again;

Passiontide

through Jesus Christ, our Lord, who on the tree of the cross did give salvation to mankind, that, whence death arose, life also might rise again; and that he who by a tree once overcame might likewise by a tree be overcome through Christ, our Lord;

Easter and Eastertide

but chiefly are we bound to praise you for the glorious resurrection of your Son, Jesus Christ, our Lord; for he is the true Paschal Lamb, which was offered for us and has taken away the sins of the world; who by his death has destroyed death and by his rising to life again has restored to us everlasting life:

Ascension Day and seven days thereafter

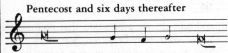

through Jesus Christ, our Lord, who after his resurrection appeared openly to all his disciples and in their sight was taken up into heaven that he might make us partakers of his divine nature;

Pentecost and six days thereafter

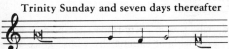

through Jesus Christ, our Lord, who ascended above the heavens and, sitting at your right hand, poured out (on this day) the Holy Spirit, as he had promised, on the chosen .disciples; whereat the whole earth rejoices with exceeding joy;

Trinity Sunday and seven days thereafter

through Jesus Christ, our Lord, who, with you and the Holy Spirit, is one God, the same in substance, equal in power and glory;

Days of the Apostles and Evangelists

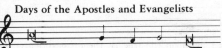

through Jesus Christ, our Lord, because you did mightily govern and protect your holy Church, which the blessed apostles and evangelists instructed in your divine and saving truth;

44

through whom with angels and arch - an - gels and with all the com-pa-ny of heaven we laud and magnify your glo-rious name, evermore prais - ing you and say - ing:

The Prayer of Thanksgiving I
(EL CULTO CRISTIANO)

Holy are you, O God, almighty and most merciful Lord, holy are you and great is the majesty of your glory. You did so love the world that you gave your only Son, that whoever believes in him should not perish but have eternal life, and you did send him into the world to fulfill for us your holy will and to accomplish our salvation.

He, our Lord Jesus Christ, on the night when he was betrayed, took bread, and when he had given thanks, he broke it and gave it to the disciples, and said:

Take, eat; this is my body, which is given for you. Do this in remembrance of me.

In the same way also he took the cup after supper, and when he had given thanks, he gave it to them, saying:

Drink of it, all of you; this is my blood of the new covenant, which is poured out for you for the forgiveness of sins. Do this, as often as you drink it, in remembrance of me.

Remembering therefore his salutary precept, his life-giving passion and death, his glorious resurrection and ascension, and the promise of his coming again, we give thanks to you, O Lord God almighty, and we beseech you mercifully to accept our praise and thanksgiving, and to bless us, your children, so that all we who partake of Christ's holy body and of his precious blood may be filled with your heavenly peace and joy; and also that we, in receiving the forgiveness of sins, together with the gifts of life and salvation, may be sanctified in body and soul and spirit and have our portion with all your saints in light.

To you, O God, Father, Son, and Holy Spirit, be all honor and glory in your holy Church forever and ever. Amen.

The Prayer of Thanksgiving II
("CAMBRIDGE")

Blessed are you, Lord of heaven and earth, who of your tender love for mankind gave your only Son, Jesus Christ, to take our nature upon him and to suffer death on the cross for our redemption. Assembled in his name and in the communion of all saints, we pray you to send down your Holy Spirit on us, and through him to sanctify and renew us in body and soul for the sake of your Son, our Savior, Jesus Christ, who

On the night when he was betrayed, took bread; and, when he had given thanks, he broke it and gave it to his disciples, saying, Take, eat; this is my ✠ body, which is given for you; do this in remembrance of me.

In the same way he took the cup, after supper, and when he had given thanks, gave it to them, saying, Drink of it, all of you; this is my ✠ blood of the new covenant, which is poured out for you for the forgiveness of sins. Do this as often as you drink it, in remembrance of me.

Remembering therefore his whole work of redemption, his conception and birth, his suffering and death, his resurrection and ascension, and looking for his glorious coming again, we here present before you the remembrance which your Son has commanded us to make, beseeching you graciously to accept this our sacrifice of praise and thanksgiving.

We pray you that so many of us as shall here receive the body and blood of our Lord Jesus Christ may be filled with all heavenly benediction and grace. Grant to us, who trust in the multitude of your mercies, our part and fellowship with all saints, not weighing our merits, but pardoning our offenses, through Christ our Lord, by whom, and with whom, and in whom, in the unity of the Holy Spirit, all honor and glory be to you, O Father Almighty, forever and ever. Amen.

The Prayer of Thanksgiving III
(APOSTOLIC TRADITION ASCRIBED TO ST. HIPPOLYTUS)

Thanks be to you, O Lord, because in these last days you did send to us your beloved Servant, Jesus Christ, to be our Savior and our Redeemer and the Messenger of your will;

Who is your Word inseparable from you;

Through whom you made all things and with whom you were well pleased;

Whom you did send from heaven into the womb of the Virgin, and who, having been conceived within her, became flesh, and was manifested as your Son, being born of the Holy Spirit and a virgin;

46

Who, when he was betrayed to his voluntary suffering, in order that he might abolish death, break the bonds of the adversary, tread Hades underfoot, give light to the righteous, establish a memorial, and manifest the resurrection, took bread, gave thanks to you, and said:

Take, eat; this is my body, which is broken for you.

Likewise also the cup, saying:

This is my blood which is poured out for you. As often as you do this, you shall do it in remembrance of me.

Therefore, having in remembrance his death and resurrection, we give thanks to you, because you have counted us worthy to stand before you and to serve you.

Gather into one, we pray you, all your holy people who partake hereof; fill them with your Holy Spirit for the confirmation of their faith in the truth; and grant that we may praise and glorify you through your Servant, Jesus Christ,

Through whom all honor and glory belongs to you, the Father and the Son with the Holy Spirit, in your holy Church, both now and forever. Amen.

POST-COMMUNION COLLECTS

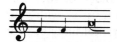

We give thanks to you, almighty God, that you have refreshed us through this salutary gift;

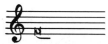

and we pray you that of your mercy you would strengthen us through the same in faith toward you and in fervent love toward one another;

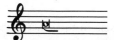

through Jesus Christ, our Lord, who lives and reigns with you and the Holy Spirit, one God,

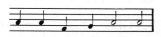

for - ev - er and ev - er.

O God the Father, Fount and Source of all goodness, who in loving-kindness did send your only-begotten Son into the flesh, we thank you that for his sake you have given us pardon and peace in this sacrament;

and we pray you not to forsake your children but evermore to rule our hearts and minds by your Holy Spirit, that we may be enabled constantly to serve you;

through Jesus Christ, our Lord, who lives and reigns with you and the Holy Spirit, one God,   for - ev - er and ev - er.

℟. A - men.

Almighty and ever-living God, we thank you most heartily that you have fed us in these holy mysteries with the body and blood of your Son, our Savior Jesus Christ; and we humbly ask you so to assist us with your grace that we may continue as true members in the mystical body of your Son and do the good works that you desire; through the same Jesus Christ, your Son, our Lord, to whom, with you and the Holy Spirit, be all honor and glory, forever and ever.

O God, as you have fed your children with the true manna, the living bread from heaven, grant, we implore you, that the body and blood of your Son may be our support throughout our earthly pilgrimage, until we reach that land where there is neither hunger nor thirst; through Jesus Christ, your Son, our Lord, who lives and reigns with you and the Holy Spirit, one God, forever and ever.

Grant, O Lord, that the lips which have sung your praise in the sanctuary may glorify you in the world, that the ears which have heard the voice of your songs may be closed to the voice of clamor and dispute, that the eyes which have seen your great love may also behold your blessed hope, that the tongues which have confessed your name may ever speak the truth, and that the bodies of all who have tasted of your Son's living body and blood may be restored to newness of life; through the same Jesus Christ our Lord, who lives and reigns with you and the Holy Spirit, one God, forever and ever.

Grant, O Lord, that what we have received with our lips we may keep with pure hearts, and that through the gift imparted to us in this present life we may hereafter receive life everlasting; through your Son, Jesus Christ, our Lord, who lives and reigns with you and the Holy Spirit, one God, forever and ever.

Grant that your Son's body and blood, O Lord, which you have given us to eat and to drink, may abide in us; and let no stain of sin remain in us, whom this pure and holy sacrament has refreshed; through the same Jesus Christ, your Son, our Lord, who lives and reigns with you and the Holy Spirit, one God, forever and ever.

Holy Father, we ask you now, by this blessed food and drink, to deliver your Church from every evil, to teach it to love you perfectly, and make it truly one, even as this bread was made from many grains of wheat to become the carrier of the body of our Savior Jesus Christ, who lives and reigns with you and the Holy Spirit, one God, forever and ever.

RUBRICS FOR THE MINISTER

Forms for Confession and Absolution and rubrics for their use are to be found on pages 54–58.

Pertaining to the Eucharist

The celebrant shall sing those portions of the service to which the congregation responds with singing. Organ accompaniment is optional.

A *Hymn of Invocation* may be sung before the Introit. If it is not convenient to sing the Introit, a metrical psalm may be sung by the congregation. (See Table, page 240.)

The *Introit,* being an entrance song, shall be said or sung by the choir or the congregation as the celebrant (with his assistants) enters the church. In place of the single psalm verse appointed in the Introit for the Day, the entire psalm from which the psalm verse is taken (or, if the psalm is long, a portion of it) may be used.

If the *Short Litany* is used in a building which is not a consecrated church, the reference to "this holy house" shall be omitted or altered. The *Kyrie* may be used either ninefold or threefold.

49

The *Gloria in Excelsis* shall be sung in festival seasons: Christmastide, Epiphanytide, Eastertide, Pentecost, and Trinity Sunday. It shall not be used during Advent and from Ash Wednesday through Holy Saturday. The congregation may kneel after the Salutation.

The *Collect* (or Collects) may be preceded by a brief period of silence. It may be read in unison by the congregation or chanted by the celebrant according to the following samples.

First Sunday in Advent

Stir up, we pray, your power, O Lord, and come,

that by your protection we may be rescued from the perils of our sins and saved by your deliverance,

    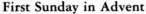

who lives and reigns with the Father and the   for-ev-er and ev-er.
Holy Spirit, one God,

Third Sunday in Lent (Oculi)

We pray you, almighty God,

look upon the desires of your servants and let the right hand of your majesty be our defense against all our enemies,

    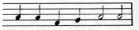

through   Jesus Christ, your Son, our Lord, who   for-ev-er and ev-er.
lives and reigns with you and the Holy
Spirit, one God,

Easter Day

Al-mighty God, who through your only-begotten Son, Jesus Christ, overcame death and opened to us the gate of everlasting life, we pray you that, as you put into our minds good desires, so by your help we may bring the same to good effect,

through   Jesus Christ, your Son, our Lord, who lives and reigns with you and the Holy Spirit, one God,   for-ev-er and ev-er.

The *Lesson,* the *Epistle,* and the *Gospel* may be read by laymen.

Announcement shall be made before each Reading as follows: "The Lesson (the Epistle, the Holy Gospel) is written in the . . . chapter of . . . , beginning at the . . . verse." After each Reading shall be said: "Here ends the Reading."

By the *Gradual* is meant that portion of the chant designated as such in *The Lutheran Hymnal,* up to the Alleluia or the Tract, as the case may be. This is sung or said after the Lesson. From the First Sunday After Easter through Pentecost the Paschal Verse shall be sung.

The *Alleluia* with its verse, or the *Tract,* is sung or said after the Epistle. If no Lesson is used, the Gradual is sung or said after the Epistle, followed at once by the Alleluia or the Tract.

The congregation shall stand for the Alleluia, since this is introductory to the Gospel. If there is a *Gospel Procession,* a hymn may be sung after the Alleluia. A procession may then be made into the nave of the church, where the Gospel may be read in the midst of the congregation.

After the Gospel has been read, those participating in the Procession shall return to their places, and the preacher shall go into the pulpit. A brief hymn or a hymn stanza may be sung after the Gospel.

When the *Sermon* is ended, the preacher shall say: "The peace of God, which passes all understanding, keep your hearts and minds through Christ Jesus." The congregation shall remain seated.

The *Creed* and the *Hymn of the Week* follow the Sermon as a reflection of the teaching of the day.

The *Offerings* of the people may be received during or immediately after the Hymn of the Week, unless they have been deposited at the door when the worshipers entered the church. (If there is no Communion, the service shall then be concluded with appropriate prayers, the Our Father, and the Aaronic Benediction.) During the singing of the Offertory the Offerings shall be brought to the altar, together with the bread and wine to be used in the Sacrament. These are to be considered as tokens of the offering of self. The monetary offerings may then be placed on a side table.

Before the *Intercessions,* the celebrant or his assistant may make mention of any special Petitions, Intercessions, or Thanksgivings that are to be offered. These shall be spoken immediately before the concluding paragraph of the Intercessions.

If the ceremony of the *Greeting of Peace* is used, the celebrant shall begin the ceremony immediately after the Pax by extending both his hands to the right hand of his assistant, saying, "Peace be with you." The assistant shall respond with the same words. The assistant shall then greet the others in the chancel, and they may, if this is desired, extend the greeting to the congregation.

Thereafter (or immediately after the Pax) the celebrant, holding a piece of consecrated bread over the chalice, and facing the people, may say, "The cup of blessing which we bless is a participation in the blood of Christ. The bread which we break is a participation in the body of Christ. O taste and see that the Lord is good! Come, for everything is ready."

The *Distribution* shall begin with the *Agnus Dei,* the celebrant receiving the Blessed Sacrament first, and after him the other ministers.

The celebrant shall customarily distribute the bread, and an assistant the wine.

When the minister gives the bread, he shall say, "The body of Christ," and when he gives the cup, he shall say, "The blood of Christ." When all have received, the celebrant may say, "The body of our Lord Jesus Christ and his precious blood strengthen and preserve you in faith to eternal life."

One or more hymns may be sung during the Distribution.

One or more Post-Communion Collects may be chanted according to the examples on pages 47 – 48.

For the *Benediction* the celebrant may sing or say:

> The Lord bless you and keep you,
> The Lord make his face shine upon you
> and be gracious to you,
> The Lord lift up his countenance upon you
> and give you ✠ peace.

Or

> The blessing of almighty God, the Father,
> the ✠ Son, and the Holy Spirit
> Be upon you and be with you all.

Pertaining to Matins and Vespers

A brief Sermon or homily may be delivered immediately before the opening Versicles or immediately after the Benedicamus.

If an Offering is gathered, this may be done during an organ Voluntary following the Sermon.

Announcements may be made, and special Supplications and Thanksgivings may be offered, before or after the Sermon or following the Benedicamus.

The officiant shall sing those portions of the service to which the congregation responds with singing.

Traditionally three Psalms are used at both Matins and Vespers. Instead of one of the Psalms, the Athanasian Creed may be used at Matins on Trinity Sunday. An Antiphon may be used with each Psalm.

The Lessons should be those designated in the Lectionary of *The Lutheran Hymnal*, pages 159 – 164, but the Lessons should not be chosen from the Psalter.

Te Deum laudamus is the proper Canticle on Sundays, except from Septuagesima to the end of Lent and during Advent. The Benedictus is proper on the Sundays of Advent, and from Septuagesima through Holy Saturday. An Antiphon may be used before and after any Canticle, but not with Te Deum laudamus. On weekdays which are not festivals, any of the lesser Canticles, including those which are printed in *The Lutheran Hymnal*, pages 120 – 122, may be substituted for a greater Canticle.

At Matins and Vespers a hymn stanza or choral selection or lesser Canticle may be substituted for the Responsory. The Responsory shall be used only after the concluding Lesson.

The Collect for the Day shall always be said first at Matins and Vespers. The concluding Collect at Matins is always the Collect for Grace, and at Vespers, the Collect for Peace. Any of these Collects may be said in unison by the congregation. They take the long termination; intervening collects, the short termination.

Matins and Vespers may be concluded with the Benedicamus if the officiant is not an ordained minister. If the officiant is an ordained minister, he may omit the Benedicamus and chant or speak the Apostolic Blessing.

A Form of Private Confession and Absolution

Private Confession shall preferably be made in the church, at or near the chancel rail.

Care should be exercised that no one overhear or disturb the penitent.

When the penitent has finished his preparation and his prayers, he shall go to the confessor, kneel down, and the confessor shall say:

Confessor: The peace of the ✠ Lord be with you alway.

Penitent: Amen.

Confessor: You have come to make your confession before God. Feel free to confess before me, a minister of his Church, the sins which trouble you.

Penitent: I, a poor sinner, confess before God that I am guilty of many sins. Especially I confess before you that . . . *(here the penitent confesses those sins which he knows and feels in his heart).* For all this I am sorry and pray for grace. I want to do better.

Together: Have mercy on me, O God, according to your steadfast love; according to your abundant mercy blot out my transgressions. Create in me a clean heart, O God, and put a new and right spirit within me.
Cast me not away from your presence, and take not your Holy Spirit from me.
Restore to me the joy of your salvation, and uphold me with a willing spirit. (Ps. 51:1, 10-12)

Confessor: God be merciful to you and strengthen your faith.

Penitent: Amen.

Confessor: *(laying his hands on the penitent)*
As you believe, so let it be. By the command of our Lord Jesus Christ, I, a called and ordained servant of the Word, forgive you all your sins in the name of the Father and of the ✠ Son and of the Holy Spirit.

Penitent: Amen.

Confessor: May the God of peace himself sanctify you wholly; and may your spirit and soul and body be kept sound and blameless at the coming of our Lord Jesus Christ. He who calls you is faithful, and he will do it. Go in ✠ peace.

Penitent: Amen.

An Order of Public Confession

This order, to be used prior to the Introit, shall be said on the First Sunday in Advent, Ash Wednesday, the First Sunday in Lent, Passion Sunday, the First Sunday After Trinity, and at other times at the discretion of the minister.

℟ *The minister turns to the altar and says:*

> In the name of the Father and of the ✠ Son and of the Holy Spirit.
> R. Amen.
> V. Our help is in the name of the Lord,
> R. Who made heaven and earth.

The minister turns to the people and says:

> Since we are assembled here to hear God's Word, (and) to call upon him in prayer, (and to receive the body and blood of Christ,) let us think of our unworthiness, confess before God that we have sinned in thought, word, and deed, and realize also that by our own strength we cannot free ourselves from our sinful nature. Therefore we take refuge in his infinite mercy, seeking and imploring his grace for the sake of our Lord Jesus Christ and say: God be merciful to me, a poor, sinful being.

✠ *The minister turns to the altar, and he and the people (kneel and) say together:*

> May almighty God have mercy on us, forgive us our sins, and lead us to life everlasting. Amen.

The minister rises, turns to the people, and says:

> Almighty God, our heavenly Father, has had mercy upon us and has given his only Son to die for us and for his sake forgives us all our sins. To them that believe on his name he gives power to become the sons of God and has promised them his Holy Spirit. He that believes and is baptized shall be saved. Grant this, Lord, unto us all.
> R. Amen.

An Order of Corporate Confession and Absolution

This order is intended to be used at confessional services apart from the Order of the Holy Communion. It envisions only those penitents being present who have specifically come to make confession and who are desirous of receiving the absolution.

If this order is used immediately prior to the service of the day, there shall be an interval of silence before the service begins.

A hymn may be sung.

✠ *The people shall rise, and the minister, facing the altar, shall say:*

In the name of the Father and of the ✠ Son and of the Holy Spirit.

People: Amen.

Minister: Almighty God, to whom all hearts are open, all desires known, and from whom no secrets are hid, cleanse the thoughts of our hearts by the inspiration of your Holy Spirit, that we may perfectly love you and worthily magnify your holy name, through Jesus Christ, your Son, our Lord.

People: Amen.

Here may follow Psalm 51 or another penitential psalm and the Gloria Patri.

Have mercy on me, O God, according to your steadfast love;
    according to your abundant mercy blot out my transgressions.
Wash me thoroughly from my iniquity, and cleanse me
    from my sin!
For I know my transgressions, and my sin is ever
    before me.
Against you, you only, have I sinned and done
    that which is evil in your sight, so that you are justified
    in your sentence and blameless in your judgment.
Behold, I was brought forth in iniquity, and in sin
    did my mother conceive me.
Behold, you desire truth in the inward being;
    therefore teach me wisdom in my secret heart.
Purge me with hyssop, and I shall be clean; wash me,
    and I shall be whiter than snow.
Fill me with joy and gladness; let the bones
    which you have broken rejoice.

Hide your face from my sins, and blot out all my iniquities.
Create in me a clean heart, O God, and put a new
    and right spirit within me.
Cast me not away from your presence, and take not
    your holy Spirit from me.
Restore to me the joy of your salvation, and uphold me
    with a willing spirit.
Then I will teach transgressors your ways, and sinners
    will return to you.
Glory be to the Father and to the Son and to the Holy Spirit;
As it was in the beginning, is now, and shall be forever and
    ever. Amen.

Then may follow a confessional address or an exhortation after the following manner:

Minister: Dearly Beloved:

Since we propose to come to the Holy Supper of our Lord Jesus Christ, it is proper that we diligently examine ourselves as Saint Paul tells us to do, for this Holy Sacrament has been instituted for the special comfort and strengthening of those who humbly confess their sins and hunger and thirst for righteousness.

But if we thus examine ourselves, we shall find nothing in us but sin and death, from which we can in no way set ourselves free. Therefore, our Lord Jesus Christ has had mercy on us and has taken on himself our nature, that in this way he might fulfill for us the whole will and law of God, and for us and for our deliverance suffer death and all that we by our sins have deserved. And to the end that we should the more confidently believe this and be strengthened by our faith in cheerful obedience to his holy will, he has instituted the Holy Sacrament of his Supper, in which he feeds us with his body and gives us to drink of his blood.

Therefore, whoever eats of this bread and drinks from this cup, firmly believing the words of Christ, dwells in Christ, and Christ in him, and has eternal life.

We should do this also in remembrance of him, showing his death, that he was delivered for our offenses and raised again for our justification, and giving him our most hearty thanks for this, take up our cross and follow him, and according to his commandment, love one another just as he has loved us. For we are all one bread and one body, just as we are all partakers of this one bread and drink from this one cup.

Minister: Humble yourselves before God, confess your sins to him, and implore his forgiveness.

Then all shall kneel. Brief silence shall be kept for self-examination.

All: O almighty God, merciful Father, I, a troubled and penitent sinner, confess to you all my sins and iniquities with which I have offended you and justly deserved your present and eternal punishment. But I am heartily sorry for them and sincerely repent of them, and I pray you of your boundless mercy and for the sake of the sufferings and death of your Son, Jesus Christ, to be gracious and merciful to me, a poor, sinful being. Forgive me all my sins and grant me the power of your Holy Spirit that I may amend my sinful life.

Then shall the minister rise and say to the penitents:

Minister: God be gracious to you and strengthen your faith.

People: Amen.

The minister shall preferably absolve the penitents individually at the altar, laying his hands on each and saying the following absolution over the first penitent and beginning with the words, "I forgive you" over the succeeding penitents, or the minister may absolve all the penitents corporately from the altar.

Minister: As you believe, so let it be. By the command of our Lord Jesus Christ, I, a called and ordained servant of the Word, forgive you your sins in the name of the Father and of the ✠ Son and of the Holy Spirit.

Penitent: Amen.

Minister: May the God of peace himself sanctify you wholly; and may your spirit and soul and body be kept sound and blameless at the coming of our Lord Jesus Christ. He who calls you is faithful, and he will do it. Go in ✠ peace.

People: Amen.

58

The Holy Eucharist
II

THE PREPARATION

¡ *A hymn may be sung.*

Minister: We are here

People: in the name of Jesus Christ.

𝄢 All: We are here because we are men — but we deny our humanity. We are stubborn fools and liars to ourselves. We do not love God nor other people as we ought. We war against life. We hurt each other. We are sorry for it and know we are sick from it. We seek new life.

Minister: Giver of life, heal us and free us to be men.

All: Holy Spirit, speak to us. Help us to listen, for we are very deaf. Come, fill this moment.

Silence for a time

THE SERVICE OF THE WORD

𝄢 *A lesson from the Old Testament may be read, followed by devotional comment, or a short hymn, or a psalm said responsively.*

A section from the Epistles should be read, followed by devotional comment, or a hymn, or a psalm said responsively.

¡ *The Gospel should then be read, perhaps in the midst of the congregation, all the people facing the reader.*

𝄢 *The Sermon should then be preached.*

𝄢 *Finally someone from the congregation, acting as deacon, may bid the Prayers and Intercessions of the assembly. The minister should speak the Prayers.*

59

THE MEAL

The First Action: Taking

Minister: If, when you are bringing your gift to the altar, you suddenly remember that your brother has a grievance against you, leave your gift where it is before the altar. First go and make peace with your brother, and only then come back and offer your gift.

Those present may greet one another with a handshake, saying, "Peace be to you."

Minister: My brothers, I implore you by God's mercy to offer your very selves to him: a living sacrifice, dedicated and fit for his acceptance, the worship offered by mind and heart. Adapt yourselves no longer to the pattern of this present world, but let your minds be remade and your whole nature thus transformed. Then you will be able to discern the will of God, and to know what is good, acceptable, and perfect.

Then an Offertory hymn may be sung, at the conclusion of which the bread and wine to be used in the Holy Communion, together with the money offerings of the people, are brought to the chancel, the bread and wine being placed on the altar, and the money on a side table.(Credence)

All: Receive, O Father, these fruits of the earth, and the products of our labors, which we offer to you in token of the sacrifice of our lives. Accept them, please, through Jesus Christ, our Lord.

The Second Action: Blessing

Minister: Lift up your hearts.

People: We lift them up to the Lord.

Minister: Let us give thanks for his glory.

People: We give thanks; we rejoice in his presence.

Minister: Thanks and praise be to you, O Father, who sent your only Son into the world to be a man, born of a woman, to die for us on a cross that was made by us.

People: He came for us. Help us to accept his coming.

Minister: He walked among us, a man, on our earth, in our world of conflict, and commanded us to remember his death, his death which gives us life; and to wait for him until he comes again in glory.

People: We remember his death; we live by his presence; we wait for his coming.

Minister: On the night when he was betrayed, the Lord Jesus took bread, gave thanks, broke it, and gave it to his disciples, saying,

"Take, eat; this is my body, which is given for you. Do this in remembrance of me." In the same way he took the cup, gave thanks, and gave it to them saying, "Drink of it, all of you; this is my blood of the new covenant, which is poured out for you for the forgiveness of sins. Do this, as often as you drink it, in remembrance of me." Therefore, remembering his death, believing in his rising from the grave, affirming his presence, now, in this place, we obey his command; we await the gift of himself.

People: Come, Lord Jesus, come.

Minister: Send down on us, O Father, the spirit of life and power, glory and love, that in this Holy Communion we may be made one with him, and he with us, and that we may remain faithful members of his body until we eat with him in his heavenly kingdom.

People: Come, risen Lord, live in us that we may live in you.

Minister: Now with all the faithful who ever were, are, and will be, with all creation in all time, with joy we sing (say):

All: Holy, holy, holy, Lord God almighty. All space and all time show forth your glory now and always. Amen.

Minister: And now, in the words of our Lord, we are bold to say:

All: Our Father in heaven:
              Holy be your name,
              Your kingdom come,
              Your will be done
                    on earth as in heaven.
              Give us today our daily bread.
              Forgive us our sins,
                    as we forgive those who sin against us.
              Save us in the time of trial,
                    and deliver us from evil,
              For yours is the kingdom, the power,
              and the glory forever. Amen.

The Third Action: Breaking

Minister (breaking the bread before the people):
       The gifts of God for the people of God.

People: Amen.

The Fourth Action: Sharing

The minister should first receive the Holy Communion himself, and then he (and his assistants) should give the Blessed Sacrament to the other communi-

61

cants. The people are urged to use this time for private prayer. The psalms, hymns, and collects printed in the service book may be helpful for this purpose.

i *When all have communed, the minister should say:*

Give thanks to the Lord, for he is good.

People: And his steadfast love lasts forever.

All: My soul, give thanks to the Lord; all my being, bless his holy name. My soul, give thanks to the Lord, and never forget all his blessings. It is he who forgives all your guilt, who heals every one of your ills, who redeems your life from the grave, who crowns you with love and compassion, who fills your life with good things, renewing your youth like an eagle's. Give thanks to the Lord, all his works, in every place where he rules. My soul, give thanks to the Lord! Give praise to the Father almighty, to his Son, Jesus Christ, the Lord, to the Spirit who dwells in our hearts, both now and forever. Amen.

Minister: Go. Serve the Lord. You are free.

People: Amen.

The Holy Eucharist
III

THE LITURGY OF THE WORD

The Opening

A hymn may be sung.

Minister: In the name of the Father and of the ✠ Son and of the Holy Spirit.

People: Amen.

Minister: Our help is in the name of the Lord.

People: Who made heaven and earth.

The Confession

Minister: Let us confess our sin to God, our merciful Father.

All: Almighty God, Father of our Lord Jesus Christ, Maker of all things, Judge of all people, we admit and confess our sinfulness. We have turned away from each other in our thinking, speaking, and doing. We have done the evil you forbid and have not done the good you demand. We do repent and are truly sorry for these our sins. Have mercy on us, kind Father, because of the obedience of our Brother, Jesus Christ, your Son. Forgive us all that is past, and with the power of the Holy Spirit move us to serve you faithfully. Set our feet upon the new path of life, and build your kingdom here through Jesus Christ, our Lord.

Minister: God has promised forgiveness of sins to those who repent and turn to him. May he keep you in his grace by the Holy Spirit, lead you to greater faith and obedience, and bring you to live with him forever, through Jesus Christ, our Lord.

People: Amen.

The Glory in the Highest

The hymn All Glory Be to God on High *or some other suitable hymn of praise may be sung.*

The Prayer for the Day

Minister: The Lord be with you.

People: And with you, his servant.

All pray silently.

The minister prays the Collect for the Day.

People: Amen.

The Readings

Appropriate lessons should now be read. They may be interspersed with psalms or hymns.

The Homily

The Intercessory Prayers

The minister presents the various intentions for which he wishes the people to pray. Each intention is introduced by the words: "Let us pray for . . ." After each intention, the people respond: "Lord, have mercy." The minister's prayers are followed by a time of silence, during which others may offer their own intentions in the same manner and with the same response from the people. After a while the minister completes the intercessions with a brief summary prayer. The people respond: "Amen."

THE LITURGY OF THE EUCHARIST

The Prayer for Peace and Unity

Minister: Let us pray as we greet one another in peace: God the Father of us all, Ruler of the universe, look from heaven upon your Church, upon all your people and upon this congregation. Give us your peace, your love, and your help. Send us the gifts of your Spirit, so that with a clean heart and a good conscience we may greet one another, not deceitfully nor hypocritically but blamelessly and purely, in the bond of peace and love. Take from us the desire to control the freedom of others, for there is only one body and one Spirit, and one faith as we have been called in one hope of our calling. Bring us to the fullness of your love in Jesus Christ, our Lord, with whom you are blessed in the unity of the Spirit, one God, forever and ever.

Here all present may greet one another with a word of peace by extending their hand(s) to their neighbors or by placing their hands on one another's shoulders.

The Offertory

While the monetary offerings of the people are being gathered, a white linen cloth may be spread on the altar, the candles lighted, and the ministers may don vestments appropriate to the celebration of the Eucharist. Bread and wine may then be placed on the altar, and the monetary gifts on a side table. A hymn may be sung during this action.

The Invitation

Minister: Luke the Evangelist wrote of our risen Lord that when he was at table with the disciples at Emmaus, he took bread and blessed it, broke it, and gave it to them. Their eyes were opened, and they recognized him. This is Christ's table. Our Savior invites those who trust in him to share the feast which he has prepared. Let us open our hearts to one another as Christ has opened his heart to us, and God will be glorified. The peace of the Lord Jesus Christ be with you all.

People: Amen.

The Thanksgiving

Minister: The Lord be with you.

People: And with you, his servant.

Minister: Lift up your hearts.

People: We lift them up to the Lord.

Minister: Let us give thanks to the Lord our God.

People: To do so is both right and proper.

Minister: We thank you, almighty Lord, that you are a God of all mankind, that you are not ashamed to be called our God, that you know us by our name, that you keep the world in your hands. For you have made us and called us in this life to be united to you, to be your people on this earth. Blessed are you, Maker of all that exists. Blessed are you, who have given us space and time to live in. Blessed are you for the light of our eyes and the air we breathe. We thank you for the whole of creation, for all the works of your hands, for all you have done in our midst, through Jesus Christ, our Lord. Therefore we praise your Majesty, almighty God, with all your faithful people; therefore we bow before you and adore you with the words:

All: Holy, holy, holy, Lord God of all living. Earth and heaven are filled with your glory. We bless your name. Blessed is he who comes in the midst of his people.

Minister: Blessed are you, almighty God, Father of our Lord Jesus Christ, blessed are you. Before the foundation of the world you chose us to be your children. You have liberated us from the power of darkness and brought us into the kingdom of your dear Son, the very image and reflection of your glory. For him the universe was made. In him we have received redemption and forgiveness of sins. On the night when he was betrayed he took bread into his hands, gave thanks, broke it, and gave it to his disciples with the words, "Take and eat; this is my body, given for you. Do this in remembrance of me." In the same way he took the cup, spoke a prayer of thanks over it, and said, "This cup is the new covenant in my blood, which is shed for you and for all for the forgiveness of sins. Each time you drink of this cup, do it in remembrance of me." When we eat of this bread and drink from this cup, we proclaim the death of the Lord until he comes. Therefore, Lord, our God, we commemorate that Christ had to suffer and die, but most of all that he is the firstborn from the dead, the firstborn of the whole creation; that glorified at your right hand, he speaks on our behalf; and that he will come to judge the living and the dead on the day which you have appointed. We pray, Lord our God, send us your Holy Spirit, the Spirit who brings to life the power of Jesus Christ. We pray that we may surrender ourselves completely to your service, and that, in the midst of this world, and before the eyes of all your people, we may live your Gospel and be the sign of your peace; that we may support and serve each other in love; that our hearts may be opened to the poor, the sick, and the dying, and to all who are in need, that so we may be the Church of Jesus Christ, united with all faithful people everywhere. Through him and with him and in him you are blessed and praised, Lord our God, almighty Father, in union with the Holy Spirit, today and all days, forever.

People: Amen.

All: Our Father in heaven:
Holy be your name,
Your kingdom come,
Your will be done
on earth as in heaven.
Give us today our daily bread.
Forgive us our sins,
as we forgive those who sin against us.

> Save us in the time of trial,
> and deliver us from evil.
> For yours is the kingdom, the power,
> and the glory forever. Amen.

The Communion

Then the Distribution shall begin, during which hymns may be sung.

The Dismissal

All: Almighty and ever-living God, we thank you for having fed us with the body and blood of our Savior Jesus Christ, assuring us thereby that we are truly members of his body, the Church. And we ask you to help us by your Holy Spirit that we may continue in this fellowship and do the good works which you desire us to do; through Jesus Christ, your Son, our Lord, to whom, with you and the same Spirit, be all honor and glory, forever and ever. Amen.

Minister: Go out into the world in peace; have courage; hold to what is good; return no man evil for evil; strengthen the faint-hearted; support the weak; help the suffering; honor all men; love and serve the Lord, rejoicing in the power of the Holy Spirit. And may almighty God, the Father, the ✠ Son, and the Holy Spirit, bless you.

People: Amen.

Immediately after the Our Father, the two following prayers may be spoken. When the minister speaks of the broken bread, he may break a piece of bread, and when he speaks of raising the cup, he may take the chalice into his hands.

Minister: We give you thanks, our Father, for the life and knowledge you have revealed to us through Jesus, your Son. To you be glory forever. As this broken bread was once scattered as seed upon the fields and after being harvested was made one, so let your Church be gathered together from the ends of the earth into your kingdom, for yours is the glory and the power through Jesus Christ forever.

People: Amen.

Minister: We give you thanks, our Father, for your holy name and for the life and immortality you sent us through Jesus, your Son. To you be glory forever. Let us raise the cup of salvation and call upon the name of the Lord. The cup of blessing for which we give thanks is the communion of the blood of Christ.

People: Amen.

A Morning Service

(MATINS)

The Versicles and the Gloria Patri

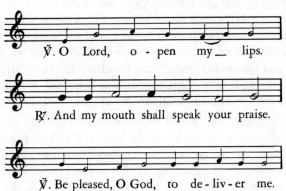

℣. O Lord, o-pen my lips.

℞. And my mouth shall speak your praise.

℣. Be pleased, O God, to de-liv-er me.

℞. O Lord, make haste to help me.

Glo-ry be to the Fa-ther and to the Son and to the Ho-ly Spir-it; As it was in the be-gin-ning, is now, and shall be for-ev-er and ev-er. A-men.

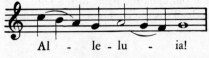

Al-le-lu-ia!

Alleluia is omitted from Septuagesima to the end of Lent. "Praise be to you" is sung instead.

68

Praise be to you, O Christ, King of e-ter-nal glo-ry.

The Invitatory

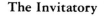

℣. The Lord is our Mak-er.

℟. O come, let us wor-ship him.

For seasonal Invitatory Versicles and Responses, see pages 78—79.

O Come, Let Us Sing

This may be sung antiphonally, as indicated.

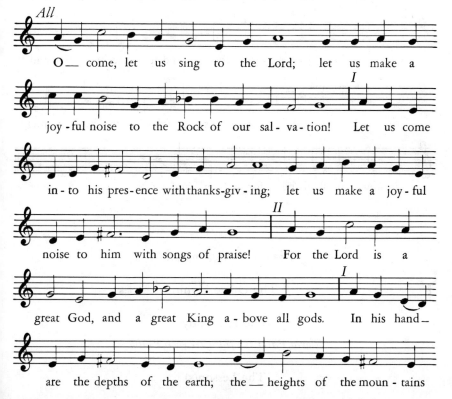

All

O— come, let us sing to the Lord; let us make a

I

joy-ful noise to the Rock of our sal-va-tion! Let us come

in-to his pres-ence with thanks-giv-ing; let us make a joy-ful

II

noise to him with songs of praise! For the Lord is a

I

great God, and a great King a-bove all gods. In his hand—

are the depths of the earth; the— heights of the moun-tains

are his — al - so. The — sea is his, and he made it; for his hand — formed the dry land. O — come, — let us wor - ship and bow down; let us kneel be - fore the Lord, our — Mak - er! For — he is our God, and — we are the peo - ple of his pas - ture and the sheep — of his hand. Glo - ry be to the Fa - ther and to the Son and to the Ho - ly Spir - it; As it was in the be - gin - ning, is now, and shall be for - ev - er and ev - er. A - men.

The Invitatory is repeated.

The Office Hymn

The Psalmody

Gloria Patri is said after each Psalm.

The Lesson(s)

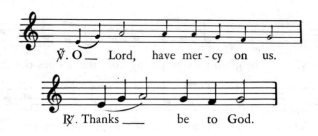

℣. O Lord, have mer-cy on us.

℟. Thanks ___ be to God.

The Responsory

(Texts on pages 95—99)

The Canticle

We Praise You, O God
(TE DEUM LAUDAMUS)

This may be sung antiphonally, as indicated.

All We praise you, O God; we ac-knowl-edge you to be the Lord.

All the earth now wor-ships you, the Fa-ther ev-er-last-ing.

I To you all an-gels cry a-loud, the heavens and all the

powers there-in. *II* To you cher-u-bim and ser-a-phim con-tin-

All ual-ly do cry: Ho-ly, ho-ly, ho-ly, Lord God of

hosts; heav-en and earth are full of the maj-es-ty of your

71

glo - ry. The glo-rious com-pa - ny of the a - pos-tles praise you. The good - ly fel - low-ship of the proph-ets praise you. The no - ble ar - my of mar - tyrs praise you. The ho - ly Church through-out all the world does ac-knowl-edge you: The Fa - ther of an in - fi -nite maj - es - ty; Your a - dor - a - ble, true, and on - ly Son; Al - so the Ho - ly Spir - it, the Coun - sel - or. You are the King of glo - ry, O Christ. You are the ev - er - last - ing Son of the Fa - ther. When you took up - on you to de - liv - er man, you did hum - ble your-self to be born of a vir - gin. When you had o - ver-come the sharp-ness of death, you did o - pen the king-dom of heaven to all be - liev - ers.

II

You sit at the right hand of God in the glo-ry of the

All

Fa-ther. We be-lieve that you will come to be

our Judge. We there-fore pray you to help your ser-vants,

whom you have re-deemed with your pre-cious blood.

Make them to be num-bered with your saints

in glo-ry ev-er-last-ing.

Or

The Song of Zechariah
(BENEDICTUS)

All

Bless-ed be the Lord God of Is-ra-el, for he has

vis-it-ed and re-deemed his peo-ple and has raised up a horn

of sal-va-tion for us in the house of his ser-vant Da-vid;

73

As he spoke by the mouth of his ho - ly proph-ets from of old,

that we should be saved from our en - e - mies and from the hand

of all who hate us; To per-form the mer - cy prom-ised

to our fa - thers and to re-mem-ber his ho - ly cov-e -nant;

The oath which he swore to our fa - ther A - bra-ham, to

grant us that we, be - ing de - liv - ered from the hand of our

en - e - mies, Might serve him with-out fear, in

ho - li - ness and righ-teous-ness be - fore him all the days

of our life.

Except during Advent, the Canticle may be terminated at this point, the Gloria Patri following immediately.

And you, child, will be called the proph- et of the

Most High, for you will go be-fore the Lord to pre-pare his ways;

To give knowl-edge of sal - va - tion to his peo - ple in the for-give-ness of their sins, through the ten - der mer - cy of our God, When the day shall dawn up - on us from on high to give light to those who sit in dark - ness, And in the shad-ow of death, to guide our feet in - to the way of peace.

All

Glo - ry be to the Fa - ther and to the Son and to the Ho - ly Spir - it; As it was in the be - gin-ning, is now, and shall be for - ev - er and ev - er. A - men.

The Kyrie and the Our Father

Lord, have mer - cy. Christ, have mer - cy.
Ky - ri - e e - lei - son. Chri - ste e - lei - son.

Lord, have mer - cy.
Ky - ri - e e - lei - son.

Our Father in heaven:
>Holy be your name,
>Your kingdom come,
>Your will be done
>>on earth as in heaven.
>Give us today our daily bread.
>Forgive us our sins,
>>as we forgive those who sin against us.
>Save us in the time of trial,
>>and deliver us from evil.

For yours is the kingdom, the power,
and the glory forever. Amen.

In place of the Kyrie and the Our Father, the Litany, **The Lutheran Hymnal,** *p. 110, or the Responsive Prayer for Morning (Suffrages), p. 79, may be said.*

℣. The Lord be with＿ you.

℟. And with your＿ spir - it.

The Collects

Before the Collect for Grace

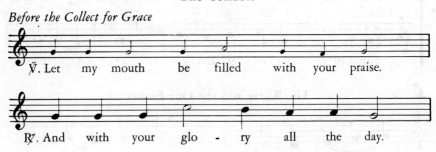

℣. Let my mouth be filled with your praise.

℟. And with your glo - ry all the day.

The Collect for Grace

O Lord, our heavenly Father, since you have safely brought us to the beginning of this day, defend us in the same with your mighty power, and grant that this day we fall into no sin, neither run into any kind of danger, but that all our doing, being ordered by your governance, may be righteous in your sight;

through Jesus Christ, your Son, our Lord, who lives and reigns with you and the Holy Spirit, one God,

for-ev-er and ev-er.

A men.

℣. Let us bless _____ the Lord.

℟. Thanks _____ be to God.

(Sermon — Offering — Collects)

The Apostolic Blessing

The grace of our Lord _ ✠ Je-sus Christ and the love of God

and the fel-low-ship of the Ho-ly Spir-it be with you all.

℟. A - men. A-men.

SEASONAL INVITATORY VERSICLES AND RESPONSES

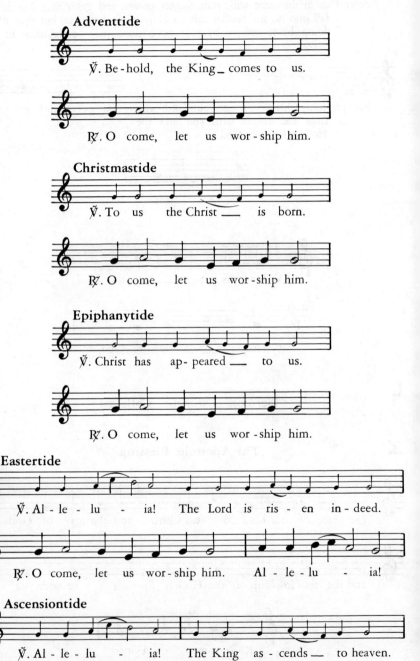

Adventtide

℣. Be - hold, the King comes to us.

℟. O come, let us wor - ship him.

Christmastide

℣. To us the Christ is born.

℟. O come, let us wor - ship him.

Epiphanytide

℣. Christ has ap - peared to us.

℟. O come, let us wor - ship him.

Eastertide

℣. Al - le - lu - ia! The Lord is ris - en in - deed.

℟. O come, let us wor - ship him. Al - le - lu - ia!

Ascensiontide

℣. Al - le - lu - ia! The King as - cends to heaven.

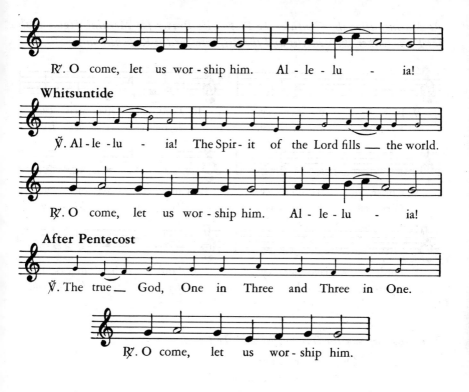

Whitsuntide

℣. Al - le - lu - ia! The Spir - it of the Lord fills __ the world.

℟. O come, let us wor - ship him. Al - le - lu - ia!

After Pentecost

℣. The true __ God, One in Three and Three in One.

℟. O come, let us wor - ship him.

THE RESPONSIVE PRAYER FOR MORNING
(SUFFRAGES)

*(The Responsive Prayer for Morning may be said at Matins, in the Morning
Prayer of the household, or alone as a brief Office. When said at Matins, the
Responsive Prayer for Morning shall immediately follow the Canticle and shall
conclude the Office.)*

*When used as a special Office, the Responsive Prayer for Morning shall begin
with an Invocation, as follows:*

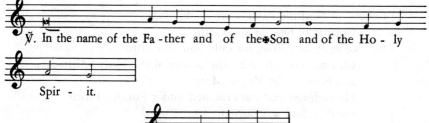

℣. In the name of the Fa -ther and of the✱Son and of the Ho - ly
Spir - it.

℟. A - men.

At Matins, after the Canticle, the Responsive Prayer for Morning begins with the Kyrie (either the Versicles and the Responses, or the Responses only):

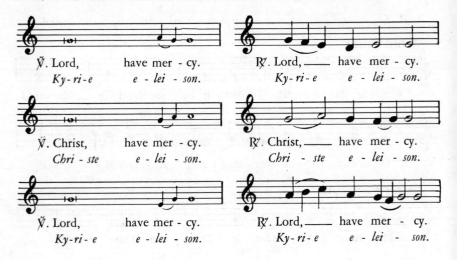

℣. Lord, have mer - cy.
Ky - ri - e e - lei - son.

℟. Lord, —— have mer - cy.
Ky - ri - e e - lei - son.

℣. Christ, have mer - cy.
Chri - ste e - lei - son.

℟. Christ, —— have mer - cy.
Chri - ste e - lei - son.

℣. Lord, have mer - cy.
Ky - ri - e e - lei - son.

℟. Lord, —— have mer - cy.
Ky - ri - e e - lei - son.

Then shall all say the Our Father and the Creed.

> Our Father in heaven:
> Holy be your name,
> Your kingdom come,
> Your will be done
> on earth as in heaven.
> Give us today our daily bread.
> Forgive us our sins,
> as we forgive those who sin against us.
> Save us in the time of trial,
> and deliver us from evil,
> For yours is the kingdom, the power,
> and the glory forever. Amen.

I believe in God the Father, the Almighty,
Creator of heaven and earth.
I believe in Jesus Christ, his only Son, our Lord,
who was conceived by the power of the Holy Spirit
and born of the Virgin Mary.
He suffered and was crucified under Pontius Pilate.
He died and was buried.
He went to the dead,
and the third day he rose again.

He entered into heaven
and is seated at the right hand of God the almighty Father.
He will come again to judge the living and the dead.
I believe in the Holy Spirit,
the holy catholic Church,
the communion of saints,
the forgiveness of sins,
the resurrection of the body,
and the ✠ life eternal. Amen.

When the Responsive Prayer for Morning is used as a special Office, the Psalm, the Lesson, and the Hymn shall follow here.

℣. I cry to you, ___ O Lord.

℟. In the morn-ing shall my prayer come be-fore ___ you.

℣. Let my mouth be filled with your praise.

℟. And with your glo-ry all the day.

℣. O Lord, hide your face from my sins.

℟. And blot out all my in-iq-ui-ties.

℣. Create in me a clean heart, ___ O God.

℟. And re-new a right spir-it with-in me.

81

℣. Cast me not away from your pres - ence.

℟. And take not your Ho - ly Spir - it from me.

℣. Restore to me the joy of your _____ sal - va - tion.

℟. And up - hold me with a will - ing Spir - it.

℣. Help us, O Lord, this day

℟. To live with - out sin.

℣. O Lord, have mercy on us.

℟. Have mer - cy on us.

℣. O Lord, let your mercy be on us.

℟. As our trust is in you.

℣. Hear our prayer, O Lord.

℟. And let our cry — come to you.

℣. The Lord be with — you.

℟. And with your — spir - it.

Then shall be said the Collect for the Day and any other suitable Collects; after which may be said the prayer here following:

We give thanks to you, heavenly Father, through Jesus Christ, your dear Son,
that you have kept us this night from all harm and danger;

and we pray you that you would keep us this day also from sin and every
evil, that all our doings and life may please you.

For into your hands we commend ourselves, our bodies and souls, and all
things. Let your holy angel be with us that the wicked Foe may

have no power — o - ver us.

℟. A - men.

℣. Let us bless ———— the Lord.

℟. Thanks ——— be to God.

83

At Matins shall be said this Blessing:

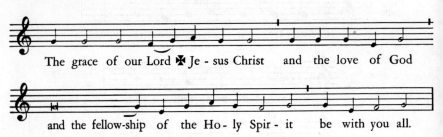

The grace of our Lord ✠ Je - sus Christ and the love of God and the fellow-ship of the Ho - ly Spir - it be with you all.

When the Responsive Prayer for Morning is said as a special Office, the following Blessing may be said:

May the Lord — Al - might - y dis - pose our days and our deeds in — his ✠ peace.

℟. A - men. A - men.

An Evening Service

(VESPERS)

The Versicles and the Gloria Patri

℣. O Lord, o - pen my — lips.

℟. And my mouth shall speak your praise.

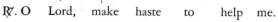

℣. Be pleased, O God, to de - liv - er me.

℟. O Lord, make haste to help me.

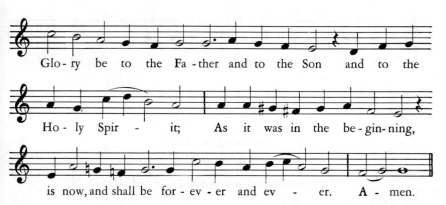

Glo - ry be to the Fa - ther and to the Son and to the

Ho - ly Spir - it; As it was in the be - gin - ning,

is now, and shall be for - ev - er and ev - er. A - men.

Al - le - lu - ia!

Alleluia is omitted from Septuagesima to the end of Lent. "Praise be to you" is sung instead.

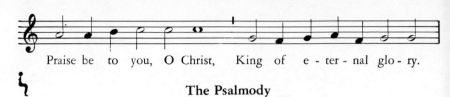

Praise be to you, O Christ, King of e - ter - nal glo - ry.

The Psalmody

Gloria Patri is said after each Psalm.

The Lesson(s)

℣. O— Lord, have mer - cy on us.

℟. Thanks——— be to God.

The Responsory

(Texts on pages 95 — 99)

The Office Hymn

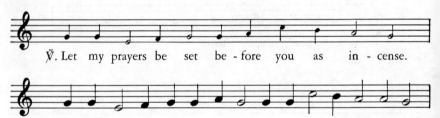

℣. Let my prayers be set be - fore you as in - cense.

℟. And the lift - ing up of my hands as the eve - ning sac - ri - fice.

The Canticle

The Song of Mary
(MAGNIFICAT)

This may be sung antiphonally, as indicated.

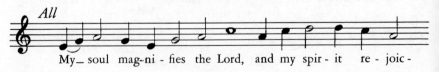

All

My— soul mag-ni - fies the Lord, and my spir - it re - joic-

es in God, my Sav - ior. For __ he has re - gard - ed the __ low __ es - tate of his __ hand - maid - en. For be-hold, hence-forth all gen - er - a - tions will call __ me __ blessed, For __ he who is might - y has done great things for me, and __ ho - ly is his __ name. And his mer - cy is on those who __ fear him, from gen - er - a - tion to gen - er - a - tion. He has shown __ strength with his arm; he has scat - tered the proud in the im - ag - i - na - tion of __ their __ hearts. He has put down the might - y from their thrones, __ and ex - alt - ed those of low de - gree. He has filled _____ the hun - gry with good things, and the rich he has sent __ emp - ty a - way.

 ## The Kyrie and the Our Father

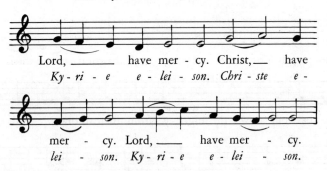

Our Father in heaven:
Holy be your name,
Your kingdom come,
Your will be done
on earth as in heaven.

Give us today our daily bread.
Forgive us our sins,
    as we forgive those who sin against us.
Save us in the time of trial,
    and deliver us from evil.
For yours is the kingdom, the power,
and the glory forever. Amen.

In place of the Kyrie and the Our Father, the Litany, The Lutheran Hymnal, *p. 110, or the Responsive Prayer for Evening (Suffrages), p. 90, may be said.*

℣. The Lord be with you.

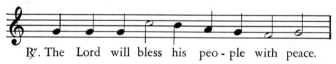

℟. And with your spir-it.

The Collects

Before the Collect for Peace

℣. The Lord will give strength to his peo-ple.

℟. The Lord will bless his peo-ple with peace.

The Collect for Peace

O God, from whom all holy desires, all good counsels, and all just works do
    proceed,

give to your servants that peace which the world cannot give, that our hearts
    may be set to obey your commandments, and also that by you,
    we, being defended from the fear of our enemies, may pass our
    time in rest and quietness,

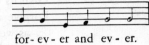

through the merits of Jesus Christ, our Savior, for- ev- er and ev- er.
who lives and reigns with you and
the Holy Spirit, one God,

R̥. A - men.

V̥. Let us bless _____ the Lord.

R̥. Thanks _____ be to God.

(Sermon — Offering — Collects)

The Apostolic Blessing

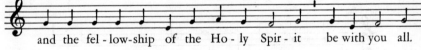

The grace of our Lord _ ✠ Je - sus Christ and the love of God

and the fel - low-ship of the Ho - ly Spir - it be with you all.

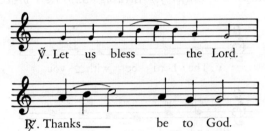

R̥. A - men. A - men.

The Responsive Prayer for Evening
(SUFFRAGES)

(The Responsive Prayer for Evening may be said at Vespers, in the Evening Prayer of the household, or alone as a brief Office. When said at Vespers, the Responsive Prayer for Evening shall immediately follow the Canticle and shall conclude the Office.)

When used as a special Office, the Responsive Prayer for Evening shall begin with an Invocation, as follows:

℣. In the name of the Fa - ther and of the ✠ Son and of the

Ho - ly Spir - it.

℟. A - men.

At Vespers, after the Canticle, the Responsive Prayer for Evening begins with the Kyrie (either the Versicles and the Responses, or the Responses only):

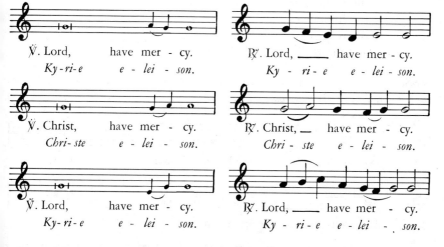

℣. Lord, have mer - cy.
Ky - ri - e e - lei - son.

℟. Lord, ____ have mer - cy.
Ky - ri - e e - lei - son.

℣. Christ, have mer - cy.
Chri - ste e - lei - son.

℟. Christ, __ have mer - cy.
Chri - ste e - lei - son.

℣. Lord, have mer - cy.
Ky - ri - e e - lei - son.

℟. Lord, ____ have mer - cy.
Ky - ri - e e - lei - son.

*Then shall all say the **Our Father** and the **Creed**.*

> Our Father in heaven:
> Holy be your name,
> Your kingdom come,
> Your will be done
> on earth as in heaven.
> Give us today our daily bread.
> Forgive us our sins,
> as we forgive those who sin against us.
> Save us in the time of trial,
> and deliver us from evil,
> For yours is the kingdom, the power,
> and the glory forever. Amen.

I believe in God the Father, the Almighty,
>   Creator of heaven and earth.

I believe in Jesus Christ, his only Son, our Lord,
>   who was conceived by the power of the Holy Spirit
>   and born of the Virgin Mary.
>   He suffered and was crucified under Pontius Pilate.
>   He died and was buried.
>   He went to the dead,
>   and the third day he rose again.
>   He entered into heaven
>   and is seated at the right hand of God the almighty Father.
>   He will come again to judge the living and the dead.

I believe in the Holy Spirit,
>   the holy catholic Church,
>   the communion of saints,
>   the forgiveness of sins,
>   the resurrection of the body,
>   and the 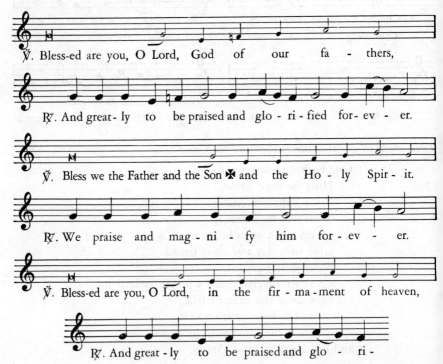 life eternal. Amen.

When the Responsive Prayer for Evening is used as a special Office, the Psalm, the Lesson, and the Hymn shall follow here.

℣. Bless-ed are you, O Lord, God of our fa - thers,

℟. And great-ly to be praised and glo - ri - fied for- ev - er.

℣. Bless we the Father and the Son ✠ and the Ho - ly Spir - it.

℟. We praise and mag - ni - fy him for - ev - er.

℣. Bless-ed are you, O Lord, in the fir - ma - ment of heaven,

℟. And great - ly to be praised and glo - ri -

fied and high-ly ex - alt -ed for - ev - er.

℣. The almighty and mer - ci - ful Lord bless and pre - serve us.

A - men.

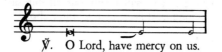

℣. Help us, O Lord, this night

℟. To live with - out sin.

℣. O Lord, have mercy on us.

℟. Have mer - cy on us.

℣. O Lord, let your mercy be on us.

℟. As our trust is in you.

℣. Hear our prayer, O Lord.

℟. And let our cry — come to you.

℣. The Lord be with — you.

℞. And with your — spir - it.

Then shall be said the Collect for the Day and any other suitable Collects; after which may be said the prayer here following:

We thank you, heavenly Father, through Jesus Christ, your dear Son, that you have kept us this day;

and we pray you that you will forgive us all our sins where we have done wrong, and keep us this night also.

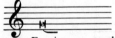

For into your hands we commend ourselves, our bodies and souls, and all things. Let your holy angel be with us that the wicked Foe may

have no power — o - ver us.

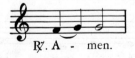

℞. A - men.

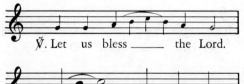

℣. Let us bless _____ the Lord.

℞. Thanks _____ be to God.

94

At Vespers shall be said this Blessing:

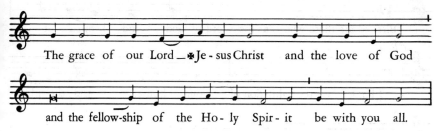

The grace of our Lord ✠ Je-sus Christ and the love of God

and the fellow-ship of the Ho-ly Spir-it be with you all.

When the Responsive Prayer for Evening is said as a special Office, the following Blessing may be said:

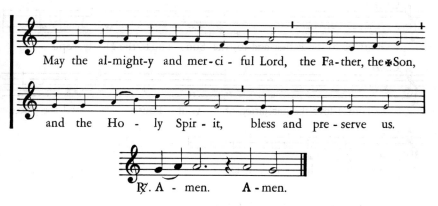

May the al-might-y and mer-ci-ful Lord, the Fa-ther, the ✠ Son,

and the Ho-ly Spir-it, bless and pre-serve us.

℞. A - men. A - men.

RESPONSORIES

Note: In adapting these Responsories to a spoken service, the cantor's parts may be spoken by the officiant, and the choir's parts by the congregation.

Throughout the Year

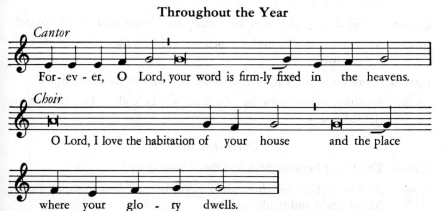

Cantor

For-ev-er, O Lord, your word is firm-ly fixed in the heavens.

Choir

O Lord, I love the habitation of your house and the place

where your glo-ry dwells.

Cantor: Bless-ed are those who hear the Word of God and keep it.

Choir: O Lord, I love the habitation of your house and the place where your glo - ry dwells.

Cantor: Glo-ry be to the Father and to the Son and to the Ho-ly Spir - it.

Choir: O Lord, I love the habitation of your house and the place where your glo - ry dwells.

Adventtide

Cantor: Behold, the days are coming, says the Lord, when I will raise up for David a righteous Branch, and he shall reign as king and deal wisely, and shall execute justice and righteousness in the land.

Choir: And this is the name by which he will be called, The Lord is our righteousness.

Cantor: In his days Judah will be saved, and Israel will dwell securely.

Choir: And this is the name by which he will be called, The Lord is our righteousness.

Cantor: Glory be to the Father and to the Son and to the Holy Spirit.

Choir: And this is the name by which he will be called, The Lord is our righteousness.

Christmastide

Cantor: The Word became flesh and dwelt among us.

Choir: And we beheld his glory, glory as of the only Son from the Father, full of grace and truth.

96

Cantor: In the beginning was the Word, and the Word was with God, and the Word was God.

Choir: And we beheld his glory, glory as of the only Son from the Father, full of grace and truth.

Cantor: Glory be to the Father and to the Son and to the Holy Spirit.

Choir: And we beheld his glory, glory as of the only Son from the Father, full of grace and truth.

Epiphanytide

Cantor: Arise, shine, for your light has come.

Choir: And the glory of the Lord has risen upon you.

Cantor: And nations shall come to your light, and kings to the brightness of your rising.

Choir: And the glory of the Lord has risen upon you.

Cantor: Glory be to the Father and to the Son and to the Holy Spirit.

Choir: And the glory of the Lord has risen upon you.

Lent

Cantor: He was brought as a lamb to the slaughter, he was oppressed and he was afflicted, yet he opened not his mouth.

Choir: He was delivered up to death that he might give life to his people.

Cantor: His abode has been established in Salem, his dwelling-place in Zion.

Choir: He was delivered up to death that he might give life to his people.

Eastertide

Cantor: Christ, being raised from the dead, will never die again; death no longer has dominion over him. Alleluia!

Choir: The life he lives, he lives to God. Alleluia! Alleluia!

Cantor: Christ was put to death for our trespasses and raised for our justification.

Choir: The life he lives, he lives to God. Alleluia! Alleluia!

Cantor: Glory be to the Father and to the Son and to the Holy Spirit.

Choir: The life he lives, he lives to God. Alleluia! Alleluia!

Ascensiontide

Cantor: Go into all the world and preach the Gospel. Alleluia!

Choir: He who believes and is baptized will be saved. Alleluia! Alleluia!

Cantor: In the name of the Father and of the Son and of the Holy Spirit.

Choir: He who believes and is baptized will be saved. Alleluia! Alleluia!

Cantor: Glory be to the Father and to the Son and to the Holy Spirit.

Choir: He who believes and is baptized will be saved. Alleluia! Alleluia!

Whitsuntide

Cantor: And there appeared to the apostles tongues as of fire. Alleluia!

Choir: And the Holy Spirit rested on each one of them. Alleluia! Alleluia!

Cantor: And they began to speak in other tongues the mighty works of God.

Choir: And the Holy Spirit rested on each one of them. Alleluia! Alleluia!

Cantor: Glory be to the Father and to the Son and to the Holy Spirit.

Choir: And the Holy Spirit rested on each one of them. Alleluia! Alleluia!

After Pentecost

Cantor: We bless the Father and the Son and the Holy Spirit.

Choir: Praise him and magnify him forever.

Cantor: Blessed are you, O Lord, in the firmament of heaven, and above all to be praised and glorified forever.

Choir: Praise him and magnify him forever.

Cantor: Glory be to the Father and to the Son and to the Holy Spirit.

Choir: Praise him and magnify him forever.

Apostles' and Evangelists' Days

Cantor: Take my yoke upon you, says the Lord, and learn from me, for I am gentle and lowly in heart.

Choir: And you will find rest for your souls.

Cantor: For my yoke is easy and my burden is light.

Choir: And you will find rest for your souls.

Cantor: Glory be to the Father and to the Son and to the Holy Spirit.

Choir: And you will find rest for your souls.

The Annunciation

Cantor: Then said Mary to the angel, Behold, I am the handmaid of the Lord.

Choir: Let it be to me according to your word.

Cantor: The Holy Spirit will come upon you. And when the angel thus made answer, Mary said:

Choir: Let it be to me according to your word.

Cantor: Glory be to the Father and to the Son and to the Holy Spirit.

Choir: Let it be to me according to your word.

Note: For the Presentation of Our Lord and for the Visitation the proper Responsory is the same as that for Christmastide.

A Service of Prayer and Preaching

I

Note: The structure of prayer in this service suggests a pattern which may well be followed in the private prayers of any individual. It may be summarized in the word ACTS: Adoration, Confession, Thanksgiving, Supplication.

A Hymn

The Sentence for the Service

(Texts on pages 110—111)

An Act of Adoration

Almighty God, before whose presence the angels veil their faces, with reverence and love we acknowledge your glory and worship you, Father, Son, and Holy Spirit, eternal Trinity. Blessing and honor and glory and power be unto our God, forever and ever. Amen.

Silence

An Act of Confession

Merciful Father, we have erred and strayed from your ways like lost sheep. We have followed too much the desires of our own hearts. We have offended against your laws. We have left undone those things which we ought to have done; we have done those things which we ought not to have done; and there is no health in us. O Lord, have mercy on us. Spare them, O God, who confess their faults. Restore those who are penitent, according to your promises declared to mankind in Christ Jesus, our Lord. And grant, for his sake, that we may live a godly, righteous, and sober life, to the glory of your holy name. Amen.

Hymn, Psalm, or Canticle

Old Testament Lesson

Hymn, Psalm, or Canticle

New Testament Lesson(s)

100

The Apostolic Creed

I believe in God the Father, the Almighty,
>> Creator of heaven and earth.

I believe in Jesus Christ, his only Son, our Lord,
>> who was conceived by the power of the Holy Spirit
>> and born of the Virgin Mary.
>> He suffered and was crucified under Pontius Pilate.
>> He died and was buried.
>> He went to the dead,
>> and the third day he rose again.
>> He entered into heaven
>> and is seated at the right hand of God the almighty Father.
>> He will come again to judge the living and the dead.

I believe in the Holy Spirit,
>> the holy catholic Church,
>> the communion of saints,
>> the forgiveness of sins,
>> the resurrection of the body,
>> and the ✠ life eternal. Amen.

A Hymn

The Sermon

The Offering

An Act of Thanksgiving

Father of all mercies, we give you thanks for all your goodness to us and to all men. We praise you for our creation, preservation, and all the blessings of this life; but above all, for your love in the redemption of the world by our Lord Jesus Christ, for the means of grace, and for the hope of glory. And we ask you, give us that due sense of all your mercies, that our hearts may be truly thankful and that we praise you not only with our lips but in our lives, by giving ourselves to your service and by walking before you in holiness and righteousness all our days; through Jesus Christ, your Son, our Lord, to whom with you and the Holy Spirit be all honor and glory, forever and ever. Amen.

An Act of Supplication
(INTERCESSION)

Almighty God, merciful Father, since you have taught us by your apostle to make prayers and supplications for all men, we pray you for your holy

101

catholic Church, that it may increase in godliness and be enriched with spiritual benefits. We pray that your ministers may be faithful, both in life and doctrine, and, setting before their eyes only your glory, may feed the Church, which you have redeemed with the blood of your Son. We pray that those who do not know you may be brought from the captivity of blindness and error to the understanding of your heavenly truth, and that those who have wandered and gone astray may be gathered and brought home to your fold.

Almighty God, from whom all thoughts of truth and peace do proceed, kindle, we pray you, in the hearts of all men, the true love of peace, and guide with your pure and peaceable wisdom those who take counsel for the nations of the earth, that in tranquility your kingdom may go forward, till the earth be filled with the knowledge of your love.

Merciful Father, since we are members of the body of Christ, we pray for those who are afflicted in any way, whether it be suffering of body, unquietness of mind, or sorrow of heart, that it may please you to give them patience and constancy until you send them deliverance out of all their troubles.

Almighty God, we give you praise and thanks for the wonderful grace and virtue revealed in all your saints, who have been chosen instruments of your grace and lights of the world in their generations. Give us grace to follow the example of their steadfastness in faith and obedience, that at the last we, with them, may inherit the kingdom prepared from the foundation of the world. Grant this, O Father, for the sake of Jesus Christ, your Son, our only Mediator, who lives and reigns with you and the Holy Spirit, one God, forever and ever. Amen.

The Blessing

The peace of God, which passes all understanding, keep your hearts and minds in the knowledge and love of God and of his Son Jesus Christ, our Lord; and the blessing of God almighty, the Father, the ✠ Son, and the Holy Spirit, be among you and remain with you always. Amen.

Note: The Sermon may follow immediately after the Opening Hymn.

A Service of Prayer and Preaching

II

Note: The structure of prayer in this service suggests a pattern which may well be followed in the private prayers of any individual. It may be summarized in the word ACTS: Adoration, Confession, Thanksgiving, Supplication.

A Hymn

The Sentence for the Service

(Texts on pages 110—111)

An Act of Adoration

Minister: Holy, holy, holy, Lord God of hosts; heaven and earth are full of your glory. Glory be to you, O Lord most high.

People: Blessed is he who has come and is to come in the name of the Lord. Hosanna in the highest.

Minister: To you all your people, from the rising of the sun to the going down of the same, cry aloud with joyful voice and say:

People: Glory be to you, O God, the Savior of all, forever and ever. Amen.

Silence

An Act of Confession

Eternal God, we confess that we have tried to hide from you, for we have done wrong. We have lived for ourselves. We have refused to bear the troubles of others and have turned from our neighbors. We have ignored the pain of the world and passed by the hungry, the poor, and the oppressed. O God, in your mercy forgive our sin and free us from selfishness, that we may choose your will and obey your commandments; through Jesus Christ, your Son, our Lord. Amen.

Hymn, Psalm, or Canticle

Old Testament Lesson

Hymn, Psalm, or Canticle

103

i

The Apostolic Creed

I believe in God the Father, the Almighty,
    Creator of heaven and earth.
I believe in Jesus Christ, his only Son, our Lord,
    who was conceived by the power of the Holy Spirit
    and born of the Virgin Mary.
    He suffered and was crucified under Pontius Pilate.
    He died and was buried.
    He went to the dead,
    and the third day he rose again.
    He entered into heaven
    and is seated at the right hand of God the almighty Father.
    He will come again to judge the living and the dead.
I believe in the Holy Spirit,
    the holy catholic Church,
    the communion of saints,
    the forgiveness of sins,
    the resurrection of the body,
    and the ✠ life eternal. Amen.

A Hymn

The Sermon

The Offering

i

An Act of Thanksgiving

Praise be to you, O God the Father, who created all things by your power and wisdom and did so love the world as to give your Son to be our Savior. Praise be to you, O God the Son, for you were made man, like us in all things except sinning, and were put to death for our trespasses and raised for our justification. Praise be to you, O God the Holy Spirit, that you have led us into all truth and do pour into our hearts the love of God. All praise and glory be to you, O God, Father, Son, and Holy Spirit, forever and ever. Amen.

An Act of Supplication
(INTERCESSION)

Let us pray for the whole Church: Gracious Father, we beseech you for your holy catholic Church. Fill it with all truth, and in all truth with all peace. Where it is in error, reform it; where it is in need, supply it; where it is right, strengthen and confirm it; and where it is torn apart, heal its divisions, through Jesus Christ, your Son, our Lord. Amen.

Let us pray for the world: Lord of all the worlds that are, Savior of men, we pray for the whole creation, order the unruly powers, crush every tyranny, rebuke injustice, feed and satisfy the nations that we, laboring together with you in freedom, may all enjoy the good world which you have made, through Jesus Christ, your Son, our Lord. Amen.

Let us pray for the sick and the sorrowing: God of all comfort, we commend to you all who are afflicted in any way, especially those whom we name in our hearts before you. . . . Grant them the consolations of which they have need, and assure them that nothing can separate them from your love, through Jesus Christ, your Son, our Lord. Amen.

Let us pray for family and friends: O God our Father, bless those whom we love, and enable us to love those whom you have blessed, that, drawing close to you, we may be drawn closer to each other, through Jesus Christ, your Son, our Lord. Amen.

Almighty God, since you have given us grace at this time with one accord to make our common supplications to you and have promised that when two or three are gathered in your name you will grant their requests, fulfill now, O Lord, the desires and petitions of your servants, as may be best for them, granting us in this world knowledge of your truth, and in the world to come, life everlasting; through Jesus Christ, your Son, our Lord, who lives and reigns with you and the Holy Spirit, one God, forever and ever. Amen.

The Blessing

The peace of God, which passes all understanding, keep your hearts and minds in the knowledge and love of God, and of his Son Jesus Christ, our Lord; and the blessing of God almighty, the Father, the ✠ Son, and the Holy Spirit be among you and remain with you always. Amen.

Note: The Sermon may follow immediately after the Opening Hymn.

A Service of Prayer and Preaching
III

Note: The structure of prayer in this service suggests a pattern which may well be followed in the private prayers of any individual. It may be summarized in the word ACTS: Adoration, Confession, Thanksgiving, Supplication.

A Hymn

The Sentence for the Service

(Texts on pages 110—111)

An Act of Adoration

Minister: Let us adore our heavenly Father, who created us, who sustains us, who loves us with an everlasting love and gives us the light of the knowledge of his glory in the face of Jesus Christ.

People: We praise you, O God; we acknowledge you to be the Lord.

Minister: Let us glory in the grace of our Lord Jesus Christ, who, though he was rich, yet for our sakes became poor; who in every respect was tempted as we are, yet without sinning; who went about doing good and preaching the Gospel of the kingdom; who became obedient unto death, even death on a cross; who died and is alive forevermore; who has opened the kingdom of heaven to all believers; who is seated at the right hand of God in the glory of the Father; who will come again, as Judge and King.

People: You are the King of glory, O Christ.

Minister: Let us rejoice in the fellowship of the Holy Spirit, the Lord, the Giver of life, by whom we are born into the family of God, and made members of the body of Christ; whose witness confirms us, whose wisdom teaches us, whose power enables us to do far more abundantly than all that we ask or think.

People: All praise to you, O Holy Spirit.

Silence

An Act of Confession

Minister: O God our Father, since you have set forth the way of life for us in your beloved Son, we confess with shame our slowness to learn of him, our failure to follow him, our reluctance to bear the cross.

People: Have mercy on us and forgive us, O Lord.

Minister: Forgive us the poverty of our worship, our neglect of fellowship and of the means of grace, our hesitating witness for Christ, our evasion of responsibility in your service, our imperfect stewardship of your gifts.

People: Have mercy on us and forgive us, O God.

Minister: Forgive us that so little of your love has reached others through us, that we have been thoughtless in our judgments, hasty in condemnation, grudging in forgiveness, slow to seek reconciliation, unwilling to help our neighbors as we ought.

People: Have mercy on us and forgive us, O Lord.

All: Have mercy on us, O God, according to your steadfast love; according to your abundant mercy blot out our transgressions. Wash us thoroughly from our iniquity, and cleanse us from our sin. Create in us clean hearts, O God, and put a new and right spirit within us.

Hymn, Psalm, or Canticle

Old Testament Lesson

Hymn, Psalm, or Canticle

New Testament Lesson(s)

The Apostolic Creed

I believe in God the Father, the Almighty,
    Creator of heaven and earth.
I believe in Jesus Christ, his only Son, our Lord,
    who was conceived by the power of the Holy Spirit
    and born of the Virgin Mary.
    He suffered and was crucified under Pontius Pilate.
    He died and was buried.
    He went to the dead,
    and the third day he rose again.
    He entered into heaven
    and is seated at the right hand of God the almighty Father.
    He will come again to judge the living and the dead.

107

I believe in the Holy Spirit,
>   the holy catholic Church,
>   the communion of saints,
>   the forgiveness of sins,
>   the resurrection of the body,
>   and the ✠ life eternal. Amen.

A Hymn

The Sermon

The Offering

An Act of Thanksgiving

Minister: Almighty God, we lift up our hearts in gratitude to you, and for all your lovingkindness we bless your holy name.

For life and health, for love and friendship, and for the goodness and mercy that have followed us all the days of our life

People: We praise you, O God.

Minister: For the wonder and beauty of the world; and for all things true and honorable, just and pure, lovely and gracious

People: We praise you, O God.

Minister: For the gift of Jesus Christ, your only-begotten Son; for the grace and truth which came by him; and for his obedience unto death, even death on a cross

People: We praise you, O God.

Minister: For his glorious resurrection and ascension to your right hand, and for his kingdom and glory and everlasting dominion

People: We praise you, O God.

Minister: For the Holy Spirit, the Counselor, the Lord and Giver of life; for your holy Church throughout the world; for all the means of grace; and for the fellowship of the redeemed in heaven and on earth

People: We praise you, O God.

All: Glory, thanksgiving, and praise be to you, O Father almighty, through Jesus Christ, our Lord, who lives and reigns with you and the Holy Spirit, one God, forever and ever. Amen.

An Act of Supplication

Minister: Almighty God, because you have committed to your people the ministry of intercession, hear us as we pray for others, and grant that our hearts may be filled with peace and love.

For your holy Church throughout all the world, that you would bestow on the ministers of your Word and Sacraments the abundance of your grace and truth and confirm your people in the faith of the Gospel, that Christ may be exalted as head over all,

People: We beseech you to hear us, good Lord.

Minister: For your people here and everywhere, that you would inspire them with love for your house, zeal in your service, and joy in the advancement of your kingdom,

People: We beseech you to hear us, good Lord.

Minister: For the nations, that you would breathe on them the spirit of peace and understanding; and for those in authority, that you would inspire in them a true desire for peace and love of concord,

People: We beseech you to hear us, good Lord.

Minister: For all our schools and colleges, and for all who teach in them and all who learn, that in humility of heart they may ever look to you, the fountain of all wisdom,

People: We beseech you to hear us, good Lord.

Minister: For all in sickness and distress, that you would give strength to the weary, relief to the suffering, and comfort to the dying,

People: We beseech you to hear us, good Lord.

Minister: For all your servants who have departed this life in your faith and fear we give you hearty thanks, and we pray you to give us grace to follow them as they followed Christ. Bring us, with them, to those things which eye has not seen, nor ear heard, through Jesus Christ, your Son, our Lord.

People: Amen.

The Blessing

The peace of God, which passes all understanding, keep your hearts and minds in the knowledge and love of God, and of his Son Jesus Christ, our Lord; and the blessing of God almighty, the Father, the ✠ Son, and the Holy Spirit, be among you and remain with you always. Amen.

Note: The Sermon may follow immediately after the Opening Hymn.

SENTENCES FOR THE SERVICES OF PRAYER AND PREACHING

General

God is spirit, and those who worship him must worship in spirit and truth.

Grace to you and peace from God our Father and the Lord Jesus Christ.

This is the day which the Lord has made; let us rejoice and be glad in it.

From the rising of the sun to its setting the name of the Lord is to be praised.

Advent

The Lord is at hand. Have no anxiety about anything, but in everything by prayer and supplication with thanksgiving let your requests be made known to God.

Christmas

Behold, I bring you good news of a great joy which will come to all the people; for to you is born this day in the city of David a Savior, who is Christ the Lord.

Epiphany

From the rising of the sun to its setting my name is great among the nations, and in every place incense is offered to my name, and a pure offering; for my name is great among the nations, says the Lord of hosts.

Lent

Rend your hearts and not your garments. Return to the Lord, your God, for he is gracious and merciful, slow to anger, and abounding in steadfast love, and repents of evil.

Jesus said: If any man would come after me, let him deny himself and take up his cross and follow me.

Passiontide

He himself bore our sins in his body on the tree, that we might die to sin and live to righteousness. By his wounds you have been healed.

Palm Sunday

Say to the daughter of Zion, "Behold, your salvation comes; behold, his reward is with him, and his recompense before him."

Easter

Blessed be the God and Father of our Lord Jesus Christ. By his great mercy we have been born anew to a living hope through the resurrection of Jesus Christ from the dead.

"I am the first and the last, and the living one," says the Lord; "I died, and behold, I am alive forevermore, and I have the keys of Death and Hades."

Ascension

Since we have a great high priest who has passed through the heavens, Jesus, the Son of God, let us hold fast our confession. Let us then with confidence draw near to the throne of grace, that we may receive mercy and find grace to help in time of need.

Pentecost

God's love has been poured into our hearts through the Holy Spirit, which has been given to us.

Trinity Sunday

O the depth of the riches and wisdom and knowledge of God! How unsearchable are his judgments and how inscrutable his ways! For from him and through him and to him are all things. To him be glory forever. Amen.

The New Year or Any Anniversary

They who wait for the Lord shall renew their strength; they shall mount up with wings like eagles; they shall run and not be weary; they shall walk and not faint.

The Office of Prime

*The Office of Prime is intended for corporate or personal use
early in the morning.*

The Versicle

V. Be pleased, O God, to deliver me.
R. O Lord, make haste to help me.

The Gloria Patri and Alleluia

Glory be to the Father and to the
Son and to the Holy Spirit;
As it was in the beginning, is now, and
shall be forever and ever. Amen. Alleluia.

(From Septuagesima to Holy Saturday, instead of the Alleluia:
Praise be to you, O Christ, King of eternal glory.)

A hymn appropriate to this Office shall be sung.

The Psalm Antiphon

Blessed are those whose way is blameless, who walk in the law of the Lord.

The Psalm

(Ps. 119:1-8 or another psalm may be said.)

Glory be to the Father and to the Son and to the Holy Spirit; As it was
in the beginning, is now, and shall be forever and ever. Amen.

The Antiphon

Blessed are those whose way is blameless, who walk in the law of the Lord.
*(Here may be added on Sunday the Psalm for the Day; on Monday, Psalm 24;
on Tuesday, Psalm 25; on Wednesday, Psalm 26; on Thursday, Psalm 23; on
Friday, Psalm 22; and on Saturday, Psalm 94.)*

The Little Chapter

(1 Tim. 1:17 or another appropriate verse may be read.)

To the King of ages, immortal, invisible, the only God, be honor and glory
forever and ever. Amen.
R. Thanks be to God.

The Responsory

V. O Christ, Son of the living God, have mercy on us.
R. O Christ, Son of the living God, have mercy on us.
V. You that sit at the right hand of the Father,
R. Have mercy on us.
V. Glory be to the Father and to the Son and to the Holy Spirit.
R. O Christ, Son of the living God, have mercy on us.
V. Arise, O Christ, and help us.
R. And deliver us for your name's sake.

The Kyrie

Lord, have mercy *or* Kyrie, eleison.
Christ, have mercy *or* Christe, eleison.
Lord, have mercy *or* Kyrie, eleison.

Our Father in heaven:
    Holy be your name,
    Your kingdom come,
    Your will be done
        on earth as in heaven.
    Give us today our daily bread.
    Forgive us our sins,
        as we forgive those who sin against us.
    Save us in the time of trial,
        and deliver us from evil.
For yours is the kingdom, the power,
and the glory forever. Amen.

The Apostolic Creed

I believe in God the Father, the Almighty,
    Creator of heaven and earth.
I believe in Jesus Christ, his only Son, our Lord,
    who was conceived by the power of the Holy Spirit
    and born of the Virgin Mary.
    He suffered and was crucified under Pontius Pilate.
    He died and was buried.
    He went to the dead,
    and the third day he rose again.
    He entered into heaven
    and is seated at the right hand of God the almighty Father.
    He will come again to judge the living and the dead.

I believe in the Holy Spirit,
the holy catholic Church,
the communion of saints,
the forgiveness of sins,
the resurrection of the body,
and the ✠ life eternal. Amen.

V. I cry to you, O Lord.
R. In the morning my prayer comes before you.
V. O let my mouth be filled with your praise:
R. And with your glory all the day.
V. Hide your face from my sins, O Lord.
R. And blot out all my iniquities.
V. Create in me a clean heart, O God.
R. And put a new and right spirit within me.
V. Cast me not away from your presence.
R. And take not your Holy Spirit from me.
V. Restore to me the joy of your salvation.
R. And uphold me with a willing spirit.
V. Help us, O Lord, this day
R. To live without sin.
V. O Lord, have mercy on us.
R. Have mercy on us.
V. O Lord, let your mercy be on us:
R. As our trust is in you.
V. Hear our prayer, O Lord.
R. And let our cry come to you.

The Collect(s)

Collect for Sundays and Festivals:

Satisfy us with your mercy, O Lord, at the beginning of this day, that in our fullness of joy all the day long we may find a true delight in singing your praises; through your Son, Jesus Christ, our Lord, who lives and reigns with you and the Holy Spirit, one God, forever and ever.

R. Amen.

Collect for Ordinary Days:

O almighty Lord and ever-living God, we pray you to direct, sanctify, and govern both our hearts and bodies in the ways of your laws and in the works of your commandments, that through your mighty protection, both here and ever, we may be preserved in body and soul; through our Lord and Savior Jesus Christ, who lives and reigns with you and the Holy Spirit, one God, forever and ever.

R. Amen.

O everlasting Jesus, who early in the morning sought strength from your Father, be with us, we pray you, at this hour as we seek his grace and mercy, that so throughout the day we may find peace and joy in all that ministers to your praise and glory.

R. Amen.

The Lord almighty order this day and all our doings in his peace. Amen.
V. Our help is in the name of the Lord.
R. Who made heaven and earth.
V. Let us bless the Lord.
R. Thanks be to God.

The Blessing

The Lord bless ✠ us and keep us from all evil and bring us to everlasting life. Amen.

The Noonday Office

The Versicle

V. Be pleased, O God, to deliver me.
R. O Lord, make haste to help me.

The Gloria Patri and Alleluia

Glory be to the Father and to the Son
and to the Holy Spirit;
As it was in the beginning, is now, and
shall be forever and ever. Amen. Alleluia.

(From Septuagesima to Holy Saturday, instead of the Alleluia:
Praise be to you, O Christ, King of eternal glory.)

A hymn appropriate to this office shall be sung.

The Psalm Antiphon

Let me not be put to shame in my hope.

The Psalm

(Ps. 119:113-120 or another psalm may be said.)

Glory be to the Father and to the Son and to the Holy Spirit; As it was
in the beginning, is now, and shall be forever and ever. Amen.

The Antiphon

Let me not be put to shame in my hope.

The Little Chapter

(Gal. 6:2 or another verse may be used.)

Bear one another's burdens, and so fulfill the law of Christ.
R. Thanks be to God.
V. The Lord is my Shepherd; I shall not want.
R. He makes me lie down in green pastures.

The Kyrie

Lord, have mercy *or* Kyrie, eleison.

Christ, have mercy *or* Christe, eleison.
Lord, have mercy *or* Kyrie, eleison.

The Our Father

Our Father in heaven:
    Holy be your name,
    Your kingdom come,
    Your will be done
        on earth as in heaven.
    Give us today our daily bread.
    Forgive us our sins,
        as we forgive those who sin against us.
    Save us in the time of trial,
        and deliver us from evil.
For yours is the kingdom, the power,
    and the glory forever. Amen.

V. O Lord, hear our prayer.
R. And let our cry come to you.

The Collect

(Another Collect may be used.)

O gracious Jesus, who at this hour did bear our sins in your body on the tree that we, being dead to sin, might live to righteousness, have mercy on us, we pray you, both now and at the hour of our death, and grant us, with all other Christian people, a godly and peaceful life in this present world and through your grace eternal glory in the life to come, where, with the Father and the Holy Spirit, you live and reign, ever one God, forever and ever. Amen.

V. Let us bless the Lord.
R. Thanks be to God.

The Office of Compline

(Traditionally said at the close of day)

The Blessing

The Lord almighty grant us a quiet night and a perfect end. Amen.

The Short Lesson

Be sober, be watchful. Your adversary, the devil, prowls about like a roaring lion, seeking someone to devour.
V. But you, O Lord, have mercy on us.
R. Thanks be to God.
V. Our help is in the name of the Lord.
R. Who made heaven and earth.

The Confession

I confess to God almighty, before the whole company of heaven, and to you, my brethren, that I have sinned exceedingly in thought, word, and deed by my fault, by my own fault, by my own most grievous fault; wherefore I pray God almighty to have mercy on me, forgive me all my sins, and bring me to everlasting life. Amen.
The almighty and merciful Lord grant to me pardon, absolution, and remission of all my sins. Amen.
V. Restore us again, O God of our salvation.
R. And put away your indignation toward us.
V. Be pleased, O God, to deliver me.
R. O Lord, make haste to help me.

The Gloria Patri and Alleluia

Glory be to the Father and to the Son
and to the Holy Spirit;
As it was in the beginning, is now, and
shall be forever and ever. Amen. Alleluia.

(From Septuagesima to Holy Saturday, instead of the Alleluia:
Praise be to you, O Christ, King of eternal glory.)

The Psalm Antiphon

Have mercy on me, O Lord, and hear my prayer.

The Psalms

(Ps. 4; 31:1-6; 134)

After each Psalm shall be said:

Glory be to the Father and to the Son and to the Holy Spirit; As it was in the beginning, is now, and shall be forever and ever. Amen.

The Antiphon

Have mercy on me, O Lord, and hear my prayer.

Hymn No. 790 or another evening hymn may be sung.

The Little Chapter

(Jer. 14:9 or another appropriate verse may be read.)

You, O Lord, are in the midst of us, and we are called by your name; leave us not, O Lord, our God.
R. Thanks be to God.

The Responsory

V. Into your hands, O Lord, I commend my spirit.
R. Into your hands, O Lord, I commend my spirit.
V. For you have redeemed me, O Lord, God of truth.
R. I commend my spirit.
V. Glory be to the Father and to the Son and to the Holy Spirit.
R. Into your hands, O Lord, I commend my spirit.
V. Keep us, O Lord, as the apple of the eye.
R. Hide us in the shadow of your wings.

The Antiphon

Save us, O Lord, waking, and guard us sleeping, that awake we may watch with Christ and asleep may rest in peace. *(In Eastertide shall be added: Alleluia.)*

The Song of Simeon (Nunc Dimittis)

Lord, now let your servant depart in peace, according to your word,
For my eyes have seen your salvation, which you have prepared in the presence of all peoples,
A light for revelation to the Gentiles, and for glory to your people Israel.

Glory be to the Father and to the Son and to the Holy Spirit; As it was in the beginning, is now, and shall be forever and ever. Amen.

The Antiphon

Save us, O Lord, waking, and guard us sleeping, that awake we may watch with Christ and asleep may rest in peace.

The Kyrie

Lord, have mercy *or* Kyrie, eleison.
Christ, have mercy *or* Christe, eleison.
Lord, have mercy *or* Kyrie, eleison.

The Our Father

Our Father in heaven:
    Holy be your name,
    Your kingdom come,
    Your will be done
        on earth as in heaven.
    Give us today our daily bread.
    Forgive us our sins,
        as we forgive those who sin against us.
    Save us in the time of trial,
        and deliver us from evil.
For yours is the kingdom, the power,
and the glory forever. Amen.

V. Help us, O Lord, this night
R. To live without sin.
V. O Lord, have mercy on us.
R. Have mercy on us.
V. O Lord, let your mercy be on us.
R. As our trust is in you.
V. Hear our prayer, O Lord.
R. And let our cry come to you.

The Collects

Visit, we pray you, O Lord, our dwellings and drive far from them all snares of the enemy; let your holy angels dwell therein to preserve us in peace; and may your blessing be upon us evermore; through our Lord Jesus Christ.
R. Amen.

Be present, O merciful God, and protect us through the silent hours of this night, so that we who are wearied by the changes and chances of this fleeting world, may repose on your eternal changelessness; through Jesus Christ, our Lord.

R. Amen.

(Especially on Saturday and during Lent)
O Lord Jesus Christ, Son of the living God, who at the hour of Compline rested in the sepulcher, and thereby sanctified the grave to be a bed of hope

120

for your people, cause us to rise again and to live with you forever; who live and reign with the Father and the Holy Spirit, one God, forever and ever.

R. Amen.

V. The Lord be with you.

R. And with your spirit.

V. Let us bless the Lord.

R. Thanks be to God.

The Blessing

The almighty and merciful Lord, the Father, the ✠ Son, and the Holy Spirit, bless and keep us.

R. Amen.

Hymn Section

Hymn Section

Savior of the Nations, Come

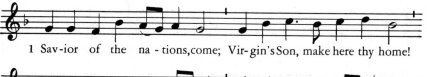

1 Sav-ior of the na-tions,come; Vir-gin's Son, make here thy home!

Mar-vel now, O heaven and earth, That the Lord chose such a birth.

2 Not by human flesh and blood,
By the Spirit of our God
Was the Word of God made flesh —
Woman's Offspring, pure and fresh.

3 Wondrous birth! O wondrous Child
Of the Virgin undefiled!
Mighty God and man in one,
Eager now his race to run!

4 God the Father is his source,
Back to God he runs his course,
Down to death and hell descends,
God's high throne he reascends.

5 Thou, the ageless Father's Peer,
Gird thy might in mortal gear;
Take on flesh to rout the wrong,
Make our flesh in frailty strong.

6 Now thy manger's halo bright
Hallows night with newborn light;
Let no night this light subdue,
Let our faith shine ever new.

7 Praise to God the Father sing,
Praise to God the Son, our King,
Praise to God the Spirit be
Ever and eternally. Amen.

A-men.

Text: Ascr. St. Ambrose (340—97); trans. sts. 1—3a, 7, William Reynolds (1812—76), sts. 3b—6, Martin L. Seltz (1909—67)
Tune: **Nun komm, der Heiden Heiland** *(Geystliche gesangk Buchleyn,* Wittenberg, 1524)
7. 7. 7. 7

Lo! He Comes with Clouds Descending

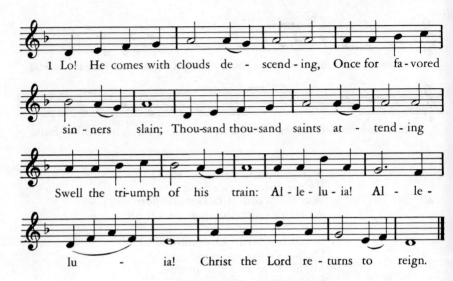

1 Lo! He comes with clouds de - scend - ing, Once for fa - vored sin - ners slain; Thou-sand thou-sand saints at - tend - ing Swell the tri-umph of his train: Al - le - lu - ia! Al - le - lu - ia! Christ the Lord re - turns to reign.

2 Every eye shall now behold him
Robed in glorious majesty;
Those who set at naught and sold him,
Pierced and nailed him to the tree,
Deeply wailing, deeply wailing,
Shall the true Messiah see!

3 Those blest tokens of his passion,
Glorified, his body bears,
Cause of ceaseless adoration
By his ransomed worshipers.
With what rapture, with what rapture
Gaze we on those sacred scars!

4 Yea, Amen! Let all adore thee,
High on thine eternal throne;
Savior, take the power and glory;
Claim the Kingdom for thine own.
O come quickly! O come quickly!
Alleluia! Come, Lord, come!

Text: Charles Wesley (1707 – 88), alt.
Tune: **Picardy** (Traditional French carol)

8. 7. 8. 7. 8. 7

Creator of the Stars of Night

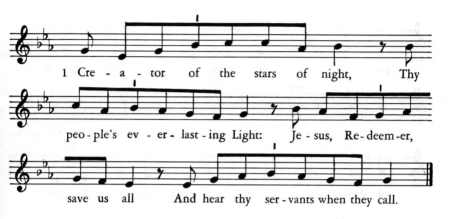

1 Cre - a - tor of the stars of night, Thy
peo - ple's ev - er - last - ing Light: Je - sus, Re - deem - er,
save us all And hear thy ser - vants when they call.

2 Thou, grieving that the ancient curse
Should doom to death a universe,
Hast found the healing, full of grace,
To cure and save our ruined race.

3 Thou camest, the Bridegroom of the bride,
As drew the world to eventide,
The spotless Victim all divine
Proceeding from a virgin shrine.

4 At whose dread name, majestic now,
All knees must bend, all hearts must bow;
All things celestial thee shall own,
And things terrestrial, Lord alone.

5 O thou, whose coming is with dread
To judge and doom the quick and dead,
Preserve us from the ancient Foe
While still we dwell on earth below.

6 To God the Father and the Son
And Holy Spirit, Three in One,
Praise, honor, might, and glory be
From age to age eternally. Amen.

A - men.

Text: 9th-century Office hymn; trans. John Mason Neale (1818—66), alt.
Tune: **Conditor alme siderum** (Sarum plainsong, Mode IV)   LM

704

Hark! A Thrilling Voice Is Sounding

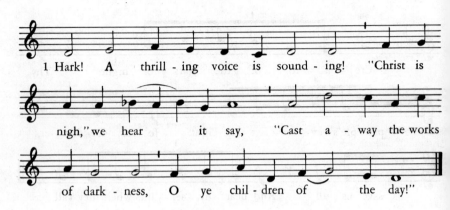

1 Hark! A thrill-ing voice is sound-ing! "Christ is
nigh," we hear it say, "Cast a-way the works
of dark-ness, O ye chil-dren of the day!"

2 Startled at the solemn warning,
Let the earth-bound soul arise;
Christ, her Sun, all sloth dispelling,
Shines upon the morning skies.

3 Lo, the Lamb — so long expected —
Comes with pardon down from heaven.
Let us haste, with tears of sorrow,
One and all, to be forgiven:

4 That, when next he comes with glory
And the world is wrapped in fear,
He may shield us with his mercy
And with words of love draw near.

5 Honor, glory, might, dominion
To the Father and the Son
With the everliving Spirit,
While eternal ages run! Amen.

A-men.

Text: 6th century, Ambrosian school, as recast for Roman Breviary; trans. Edward Caswall
(1814 — 78) †
Tune: **Freuen wir uns alle**, Michael Weisse (c. 1480 — 1534)   8. 7. 8. 7

Come, Thou Long-Expected Jesus

1 Come, thou long-ex-pect-ed Je-sus, Born to set thy
peo-ple free; From our fears and sins re-lease us;
Let us find our rest in thee. Is-rael's Strength and
Con-so-la-tion, Hope of all the earth thou art,
Dear De-sire of ev-ery na-tion, Joy of ev-ery long-ing heart.

2 Born thy people to deliver;
Born a child and yet a king!
Born to reign in us forever,
Now thy gracious kingdom bring.
By thine own eternal Spirit
Rule in all our hearts alone;
By thine all-sufficient merit
Raise us to thy glorious throne.

Text: Charles Wesley (1707—88)
Tune: **Jefferson** (*Southern Harmony*, 1835)

8. 7. 8. 7. D

How beautiful upon the mountains are the feet of him who brings good tidings, who publishes peace, who brings good tidings of good, who publishes salvation, who says to Zion, "Your God reigns." Isaiah 52:7

706

O Savior, Rend the Heavens Wide

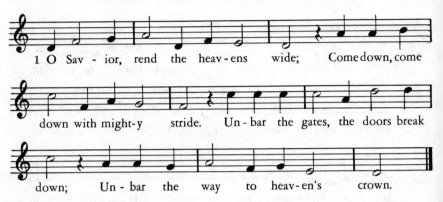

1 O Sav - ior, rend the heav - ens wide; Come down, come down with might-y stride. Un - bar the gates, the doors break down; Un - bar the way to heav-en's crown.

2 O Father, dew from heaven send;
As gentle dew, O Son, descend.
Drop down, you clouds, and torrents bring;
To Jacob's line rain down the King.

3 O earth, in flowering bud be seen;
Clothe hill and dale in garb of green.
O earth, bring forth this Blossom rare;
O Savior, rise from meadow fair.

4 O Fount of hope, how long, how long?
When wilt thou come with comfort strong?
O come, O come, high heaven forego;
Console us in our vale of woe.

5 O Morning Star, O radiant Sun,
When will our hearts behold thy dawn?
O Sun, arise; without thy light
We grope in gloom and dark of night.

6 Here dreadful doom upon us lies;
Death looms so grim before our eyes.
O come, lead us with mighty hand
From exile to our fatherland.

7 There will we all our praises bring
Ever to thee, our Savior King;
There will we laud thee and adore
Forever and forevermore.

Text: Old German Catholic spiritual song, Cologne, 1623; trans. Martin L. Seltz (1909—67)
Tune: O Heiland, reiss die Himmel auf, Augsburg, 1666
LM

The King Shall Come When Morning Dawns

1 The King shall come when morn-ing dawns And light tri - um-phant

breaks, When beau-ty gilds the east-ern hills And life to joy a-wakes:

2 Not as of old a little child,
   To bear and fight and die,
   But crowned with glory like the sun
   That lights the morning sky.

3 O brighter than the rising morn
   When he, victorious, rose
   And left the lonesome place of death,
   Despite the rage of foes:

4 O brighter than that glorious morn
   Shall this fair morning be,
   When Christ, our King, in beauty comes
   And we his face shall see!

5 The King shall come when morning dawns
   And light and beauty brings.
   Hail, Christ the Lord! Thy people pray:
   Come quickly, King of kings.

Text: John Brownlie (1859−1925), cento
Tune: **Consolation** (*Kentucky Harmony*, 1816)   **CM**

There shall come forth a shoot from the stump
of Jesse, and a branch shall grow out of his roots.
And the Spirit of the Lord shall rest upon him,
the spirit of wisdom and understanding, the
spirit of counsel and might, the spirit of knowledge and the fear of the Lord. Isaiah 11:1-2

We Praise, O Christ, Your Holy Name

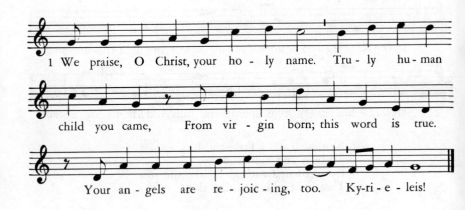

1 We praise, O Christ, your ho - ly name. Tru - ly hu - man
child you came, From vir - gin born; this word is true.
Your an - gels are re - joic - ing, too. Ky-ri - e - leis!

2 Now in the manger one may see
   God's Son from eternity,
   The Gift from God's eternal throne
   Here clothed in our poor flesh and bone.
      Kyrieleis!

3 The Virgin Mother lulls to sleep
   Him who rules the cosmic deep;
   This Infant is the Lord of day,
   Whom all the turning worlds obey.
      Kyrieleis!

4 The Light Eternal, breaking through,
   Made the world to gleam anew;
   His beams have pierced the core of night,
   He makes us children of the light,
      Kyrieleis!

5 The Prince, God's very Son, came here,
   Guest among the sons of fear.
   His banner leads us out of woe,
   And to his royal hall we go.
      Kyrieleis!

6 To earth he came so poor to bring
   Great compassion as our King
   That rich in glory we might stand
   With angels in the heavenly land.
      Kyrieleis!

7 Such grace toward us now fills with light
  Length and breadth and depth and height!
  O endless ages, raise your voice;
  O Christendom, rejoice, rejoice!
    Kyrieleis!

Text: St. 1, c. 1370; sts. 2 – 7, Martin Luther (1483 – 1546); trans. F. Samuel Janzow (1913 –)
Tune: **Gelobet seist du, Jesu Christ** (14th century; *Enchiridion,* Erfurt, 1524)   8. 7. 8. 8. 4

The Christian Year *CHRISTMASTIDE*   **709**
Hymn of the Week, Second Sunday After Christmas

From East to West, from Shore to Shore

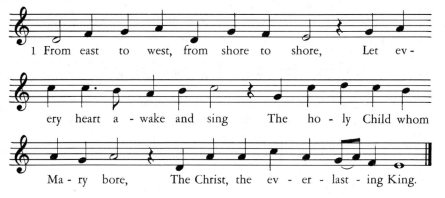

1 From east to west, from shore to shore, Let ev-ery heart a-wake and sing The ho-ly Child whom Ma-ry bore, The Christ, the ev-er-last-ing King.

2 Behold, the world's Creator wears
  The form and fashion of a slave;
  Our very flesh our Maker shares,
  His fallen creature, man, to save.

3 For this how wondrously he wrought!
  A maiden, in her lowly place,
  Became, in ways beyond all thought,
  The chosen vessel of his grace.

4 And while the angels in the sky
  Sang praise above the silent field,
  To shepherds poor, the Lord most high,
  The one great Shepherd, was revealed.

5 All glory for this blessèd morn
  To God the Father ever be;
  All praise to thee, O Virgin-born,
  All praise, O Holy Ghost, to thee. Amen.

A-men.

Text: Coelius Sedulius, d. 450, cento; trans. John Ellerton (1826 – 93)
Tune: **Christum wir sollen loben schon** (*Enchiridion,* Erfurt, 1524)   LM

710

O Come, All Ye Faithful

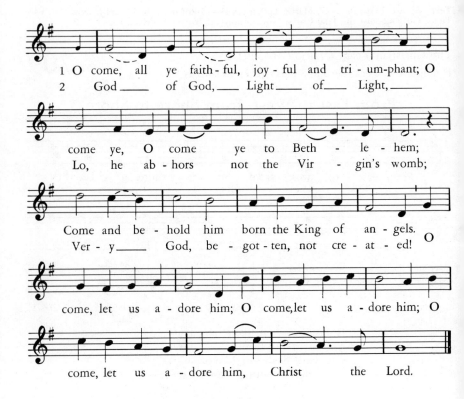

1 O come, all ye faith-ful, joy-ful and tri-um-phant; O
2 God of God, Light of Light,

come ye, O come ye to Beth - le - hem;
Lo, he ab - hors not the Vir - gin's womb;

Come and be - hold him born the King of an - gels. O
Ver - y God, be - got-ten, not cre - at - ed!

come, let us a - dore him; O come, let us a - dore him; O

come, let us a - dore him, Christ the Lord.

3 Sing, choirs of angels, sing in exultation;
Sing, all ye citizens of heaven above:
Glory to God in the highest!

4 Yea, Lord, we greet thee, born this happy morning;
Jesus, to thee be glory given;
Word of the Father, now in flesh appearing!

(If desired, the following stanzas in Latin may also be sung.)

1 Adeste, fideles, laeti triumphantes,
Venite, venite in Bethlehem;
Natum videte Regem angelorum.

Refrain: Venite, adoremus; venite, adoremus;
Venite, adoremus Dominum.

2 Deum de Deo, lumen de lumine,
   Gestant puellae viscera;
   Deum verum, genitum, non factum.

Text: Anonymous 18th-century carol, cento; trans. Frederick Oakeley (1802 – 80), alt.
Tune: **Adeste fideles** (18th century)   Irregular

Angels We Have Heard on High

1 An - gels we have heard on high, Sweet-ly sing - ing o'er the plains,
And the moun-tains in re - ply Ech - o - ing their joy - ous strains:
Glo - - - - ri - a in ex - cel - sis De - o; Glo - - - - ri - a in ex - cel - sis De - o!

2 Shepherds, why this jubilee?
   Why your joyous strains prolong?
   What the gladsome tidings be
   Which inspire your heavenly song?

3 Come to Bethlehem and see
   Him whose birth the angels sing;
   Come, adore on bended knee
   Christ the Lord, the newborn King.

4 Glory to the Father be,
   Glory, Virgin-born, to thee,
   Glory to the Holy Ghost,
   Praised by men and heavenly host:

Text: 18th-century French carol, cento
Tune: **Gloria** (Traditional French carol)   7. 7. 7. 7 with refrain

Let All Together Praise Our God

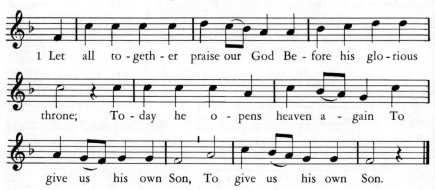

1 Let all to-geth-er praise our God Be-fore his glo-rious throne; To-day he o-pens heaven a-gain To give us his own Son, To give us his own Son.

2 The Father sends him from his throne
To be an infant small
And lie here poorly mangered now
In this cold, dismal stall.

3 Within an earthborn form he hides
His all-creating light;
To serve us all he humbly cloaks
The splendor of his might.

4 He undertakes a great exchange,
Puts on our human frame,
And in return gives us his realm,
His glory, and his name.

5 He is a servant, I a lord:
How great a mystery!
How strong the tender Christ Child's love!
No truer friend than he.

6 He is the Key, and he the Door
To blessed Paradise;
The angel bars the way no more,
To God our praises rise.

7 Your grace in lowliness revealed,
Lord Jesus, we adore,
And praise to God the Father yield
And Spirit evermore;
We praise you evermore. Amen.

A-men.

Text: Nikolaus Herman (c. 1480–1561), cento; trans. F. Samuel Janzow (1913–)
Tune: **Lobt Gott, ihr Christen allzugleich**, Nikolaus Herman (1554)   8. 6. 8. 6. 6

From Shepherding of Stars That Gaze

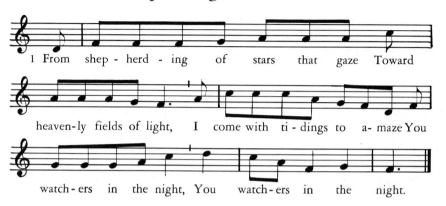

1 From shep-herd-ing of stars that gaze Toward heaven-ly fields of light, I come with ti-dings to a-maze You watch-ers in the night, You watch-ers in the night.

2 Your Shepherd-King from starlit hall
Bends down to weary lands,
Lies mangered low in cattle stall.
Go touch his infant hands.

3 This night your King brings from afar
The Virgin's lullaby,
The Wise Men's faith, a guiding star,
And love from God most high.

4 He shepherds from the thistled place
The flock by thickets torn,
His piercèd hand heals all your race —
Sore wounded by the thorn.

5 Cradle the Christ Child, and with songs
Bind up the hearts of men:
To Shepherd-Healer-King let throngs
Sing glorias again.

Text: F. Samuel Janzow (*Lutheran Education*, November 1963)
Tune: **Shepherding**, Richard Hillert (*Lutheran Education*, November 1963)   8. 6. 8. 6. 6

The grace of God has appeared for the salvation of all men, training us to renounce irreligion and worldly passions, and to live sober, upright, and godly lives in this world, awaiting our blessed hope, the appearing of the glory of our great God and Savior Jesus Christ, who gave himself for us. Titus 2:11-14

In dulci jubilo

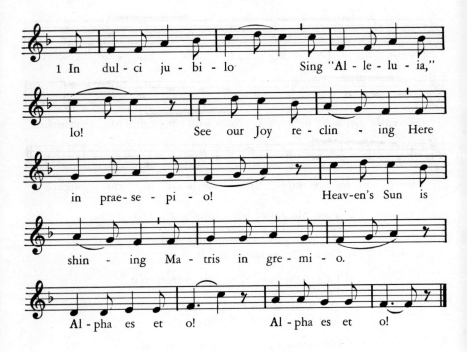

1 In dul - ci ju - bi - lo   Sing "Al - le - lu - ia,"
lo!   See our Joy re - clin - ing Here
in prae - se - pi - o!   Heav-en's Sun is
shin - ing Ma - tris in gre - mi - o.
Al - pha es et o!   Al - pha es et o!

2 O Jesu parvule,
  For thee I long alway!
  Heal my heart and spirit,
  O puer optime,
  Through thy saving merit,
  O princeps gloriae,
  Trahe me post te!

3 O Patris caritas!
  O Nati lenitas!
  Sin our soul was staining
  Per nostra crimina,
  Came the Christ regaining
  Caelorum gaudia.
  O that we were there!

4 Ubi sunt gaudia?
  Where else but there on high,
  Where the angels, singing
  Nova cantica,
  Joyous bells are ringing
  In Regis curia?
  O that we were there!

Text: 14th-century Latin-German macaronic carol; trans. Martin L. Seltz (1909 – 67)
Tune: **In dulci jubilo** (14th-century carol; Klug's *Geistliche Lieder*, Wittenberg, 1535)
                                     6. 6. 6. 6. 6. 6. 5. 5

O Little Town of Bethlehem

1 O lit - tle town of Beth - le - hem, How still we see thee lie! A - bove thy deep and dream - less sleep The si - lent stars go by; Yet in thy dark streets shin - eth The ev - er - last - ing Light; The hopes and fears of all the years Are met in thee to - night.

2 For Christ is born of Mary,
And gathered all above
While mortals sleep, the angels keep
Their watch of wondering love.
O morning stars, together
Proclaim the holy birth,
And praises sing to God, the King,
And peace to men on earth.

3 How silently, how silently
The wondrous Gift is given!
So God imparts to human hearts
The blessings of his heaven.
No ear may hear his coming,
But in this world of sin,
Where meek souls will receive him, still
The dear Christ enters in.

4 O holy Child of Bethlehem,
Descend to us, we pray;
Cast out our sin and enter in,
Be born in us today.
We hear the Christmas angels
The great glad tidings tell;
O come to us, abide with us,
Our Lord Immanuel!

Text: Phillips Brooks (1835 – 93), cento
Tune: **Forest Green** (Traditional English tune)

8. 6. 8. 6. 7. 6. 8. 6

Gentle Mary Laid Her Child

1 Gen-tle Ma-ry laid her Child Low-ly in a man-ger;
There he lay, the Un-de-filed, To the world a stran-ger.
Such a Babe in such a place, Can he be the Sav-ior?
Ask the saved of all the race Who have found his fa-vor.

2 Angels sang about his birth,
Wise men sought and found him;
Heaven's star shone brightly forth
Glory all around him.
Shepherds saw the wondrous sight,
Heard the angels singing;
All the plains were lit that night,
All the hills were ringing.

3 Gentle Mary laid her Child
Lowly in a manger;
He is still the Undefiled,
But no more a stranger.
Son of God of humble birth,
Beautiful the story;
Praise his name in all the earth;
Hail! the King of glory!

Text: Joseph Simpson Cook (1859—1933)
Tune: **Tempus adest floridum** (*Piae Cantiones*, 1582)   7. 6. 7. 6. D

This Little Babe So Few Days Old

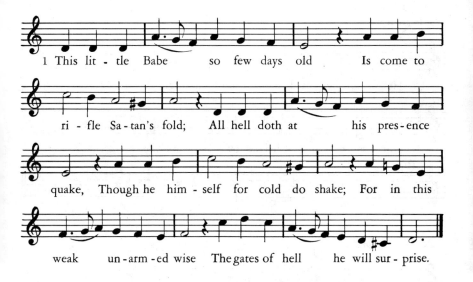

1 This lit - tle Babe   so few days old   Is come to
ri - fle Sa - tan's fold;   All hell doth at   his pres - ence
quake, Though he him - self for cold do shake; For in this
weak   un - arm - ed wise   The gates of hell   he will sur - prise.

2 With tears he fights and wins the field
His naked breast stands for a shield;
His battering shot are babish cries,
His arrows looks of weeping eyes,
His martial ensigns Cold and Need,
And feeble Flesh his warrior's steed.

3 His camp is pitchèd in a stall,
His bulwark but a broken wall;
The crib his trench, haystalks his stakes;
And thus, as sure his foe to wound,
The angels' trumps alarum sound.

4 My soul, with Christ join thou in fight;
Stick to the tents that he hath pight.*
Within his crib is surest ward;
This little Babe will be thy Guard.
If thou wilt foil thy foes with joy,
Then flit not from this heavenly Boy.
* pight = pitched, set up

Text: Robert Southwell (c. 1561 – 95)
Tune: **Das neugeborne Kindelein**, Melchior Vulpius (c. 1570 – 1615)   8. 8. 8. 8. 8. 8

718

The Quempas Celebration

Quem pastores

In groups

He whom shep-herd men came prais-ing, Awed by heav - en light a blaz-ing, Cheered by an - gel news a-maz-ing: King of glo - ry Christ is born!

Nunc angelorum

Choir

The glo-rious an - gels came to-day A - glow with light in-to the night of dark-ness deep, To shep-herds who by moon's bright ray Did in the field o'er sheep their si - lent vi-gil keep. "Joy, great joy and tid - ings glad we bring from heaven re - sound-ing, For you, for you and all the world a - bound - ing."

Resonet in laudibus

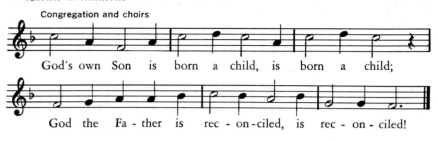

Congregation and choirs

God's own Son is born a child, is born a child;

God the Fa - ther is rec - on - ciled, is rec - on - ciled!

2 GROUP A He whom sages, westward faring,
          B Myrrh and gold and incense bearing,
          C Humbly worshiped, offerings sharing:
          D Judah's Lion reigns this morn!
  CHOIR: "God's majesty has come to earth
           And sent his only Son to you in humankind;
           A chosen virgin gave him birth,
           In David's town the holy Infant you will find,
           Lying helpless in a manger, poor and bare and lowly,
           To set you free from all your sorrow wholly."
  ALL: God's own Son . . .

3 GROUP A Sing with Mary, maiden mother;
          B Laud her Son, our newborn Brother;
          C Angel ranks, lead one another,
          D Hailing him in holy joy!
  CHOIR: Then sang the angels this refrain:
           "To God on high alone give praise and glory,
           And peace on earth again shall reign;
           Let all mankind with gladness heed this story
           And rejoice in his good will." The Savior came in meekness
           For you, for you to bear your flesh in weakness.
  ALL: God's own Son . . .

4 GROUP A To our King, God ever-reigning,
          B Yet of Mary manhood gaining,
          C Heavenly gifts for us obtaining,
          D Raise your hymns of homage high!
  CHOIR: The wondering shepherds said, "Behold,
           Let us now go with all good speed to Bethlehem
           To see this thing the Lord has told.
           The cattle leave; he will indeed take care of them."
           There they found the Wonder Babe, in lowly swaddling
              clothes lying,
           Though all the world with his free grace supplying.
  ALL: God's own Son . . .

Note: If the Quempas Celebration is not desired in its entirety, the four stanzas of *Quem pastores* assigned to the four groups may be sung as a separate carol, and the four stanzas of *Nunc angelorum* assigned to the choir may be sung as a separate carol. The refrain assigned to *All* is then omitted.

Texts: 14th-century carols; trans. Martin L. Seltz (1909–67), based on Winfred Douglas; Herbert Bouman (1908–)
Tunes: **Quem pastores, Nunc angelorum,** and **Resonet in laudibus** (14th-century carols)
                                                      8. 8. 8. 7

What Child Is This

1 What Child is this, who, laid to rest, On Mary's lap is sleeping? Whom angels greet with anthems sweet While shepherds watch are keeping? This, this is Christ the King, Whom shepherds guard and angels sing: Haste, haste to bring him laud, The Babe, the Son of Mary!

2 Why lies he in such mean estate
Where ox and ass are feeding?
Good Christian, fear; for sinners here
The silent Word is pleading.
Nails, spear shall pierce him through,
The cross be borne for me, for you:
Hail, hail the Word made flesh,
The Babe, the Son of Mary!

3 So bring him incense, gold, and myrrh,
Come peasant, king, to own him.
The King of kings salvation brings;
Let loving hearts enthrone him.
Raise, raise the song on high,
The Virgin sings her lullaby:
Joy, joy, for Christ is born,
The Babe, the Son of Mary!

Text: William Chatterton Dix (1837–98)
Tune: **Greensleeves** (16th-century English ballad)

8. 7. 8. 7. 6. 8. 6. 7

Who Are These That Earnest Knock

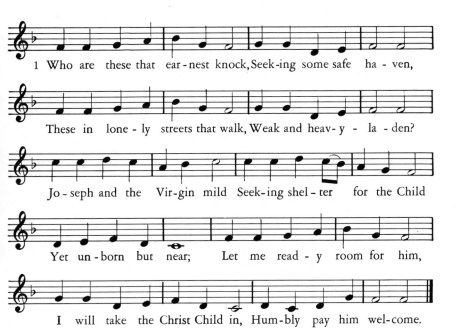

1 Who are these that ear-nest knock, Seek-ing some safe ha-ven,

These in lone-ly streets that walk, Weak and heav-y-la-den?

Jo-seph and the Vir-gin mild Seek-ing shel-ter for the Child

Yet un-born but near; Let me read-y room for him,

I will take the Christ Child in, Hum-bly pay him wel-come.

2 Who is this that docile lies
In a lowly cradle?
Who is this that dignifies
This rude, common stable?
Christ the everliving Lord,
By the angel hosts adored,
Come to meet his death.
O Redeemer of my sin,
O how great thy love has been
To be born to save me.

3 Who are these that silent stand
Filled with holy wonder,
Proselyte and pilgrim-band,
Thousand without number?
Shepherds, sages, saints whose eyes
See the newborn Sacrifice
With discerning faith.
All unworthy, yet make me
One who sees his majesty,
One who kneels adoring.

Text: Henry L. Lettermann (1932–)
Tune: **Dies est laetitiae**, variant (15th-century German tune)   7. 6. 7. 6. 7. 7. 5. 7. 7. 6

Lord, thou hast been our dwelling place in all
generations. Before the mountains were brought
forth, or ever thou hadst formed the earth and
the world, from everlasting to everlasting thou
art God. Psalm 90:1-2

Of the Father's Love Begotten

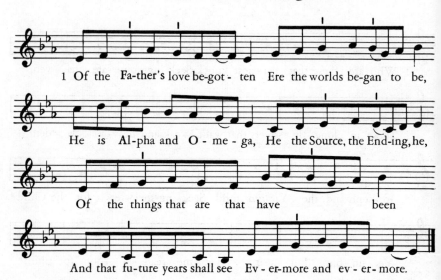

1 Of the Fa-ther's love be-got-ten Ere the worlds be-gan to be,

He is Al-pha and O-me-ga, He the Source, the End-ing, he,

Of the things that are that have been

And that fu-ture years shall see Ev-er-more and ev-er-more.

2 O that birth forever blessèd
When the Virgin, full of grace,
By the Holy Ghost conceiving,
Bore the Savior of our race,
And the Babe, the world's
  Redeemer,
First revealed his sacred face,
Evermore and evermore.

3 O ye heights of heaven, adore him;
Angel hosts, his praises sing;
Powers, dominions, bow before
  him
And extol our God and King.
Let no tongue on earth be silent,
Every voice in concert ring
Evermore and evermore.

4 Christ, to thee, with God the Father
And, O Holy Ghost, to thee,
Hymn and chant and high thanksgiving
And unending praises be,
Honor, glory, and dominion,
And eternal victory
Evermore and evermore. Amen.

A - men.

Text: Aurelius Prudentius (348 – c. 413), cento; st. 5, anonymous; trans. John Mason Neale (1818 – 66), adapted 1859 by Henry W. Baker (1821 – 77)
Tune: **Divinum mysterium** (13th-century plainsong, Mode V)   8. 7. 8. 7. 8. 7. 7

Pray the Lord our God to give you a strong faith
so that you may keep this teaching. Martin Luther
(1533)

The Only Son from Heaven

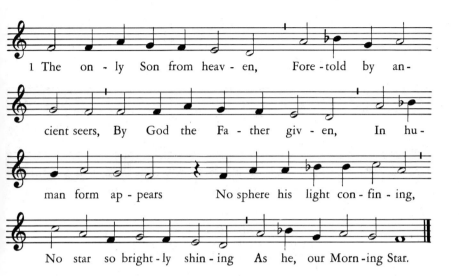

1 The on - ly Son from heav - en, Fore - told by an -
cient seers, By God the Fa - ther giv - en, In hu -
man form ap - pears No sphere his light con - fin - ing,
No star so bright - ly shin - ing As he, our Morn - ing Star.

2 O time of God appointed,
O bright and holy morn!
He comes, the King anointed,
The Christ, the Virgin-born,
Grim death to vanquish for us,
To open heaven before us
And bring us life again.

3 O Lord, our hearts awaken
To know and love thee more,
In faith to stand unshaken,
In spirit to adore,
That we still heavenward hasting,
Yet here thy joy foretasting,
May reap its fullness there.

4 O Father, here before thee,
With God the Holy Ghost,
And Jesus, we adore thee,
Thou Pride of angel-host:
Before thee mortals lowly
Cry, "Holy, holy, holy,
One God in Persons Three!" Amen.

A - men.

Text: Elizabeth Cruciger (c. 1500–35), cento; trans. Arthur T. Russell (1806–74), alt.
Tune: **Herr Christ, der einig Gotts Sohn** (15th-century tune; Erfurt, 1524) 7. 6. 7. 6. 7. 7. 6

From him and through him and to him are all things. To him be glory forever. Amen. Romans 11:36

O Wondrous Type! O Vision Fair

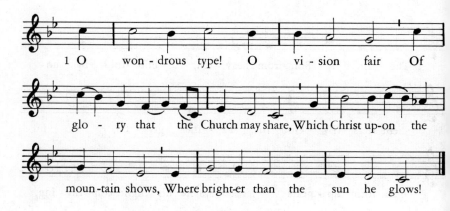

1 O won - drous type! O vi - sion fair Of
glo - ry that the Church may share, Which Christ up-on the
moun-tain shows, Where bright-er than the sun he glows!

2 With Moses and Elijah nigh
The incarnate Lord holds converse high;
And from the cloud the Holy One
Bears record to the only Son.

3 With shining face and bright array,
Christ deigns to manifest today
What glory shall be theirs above
Who joy in God with perfect love.

4 And faithful hearts are raised on high
By this great vision's mystery;
For which in joyful strains we raise
The voice of prayer, the hymn of praise.

5 O Father, with the eternal Son,
And Holy Spirit, ever One,
Vouchsafe to bring us by thy grace
To see thy glory face to face. Amen.

A - men.

Text: 15th-century Office hymn; trans. John Mason Neale (1818—66), cento, alt.
Tune: **Deo gracias** (15th-century English tune)

LM

If anyone is in Christ, he is a new creation; the
old has passed away, behold, the new has come.
2 Corinthians 5:17

Down from the Mount of Glory

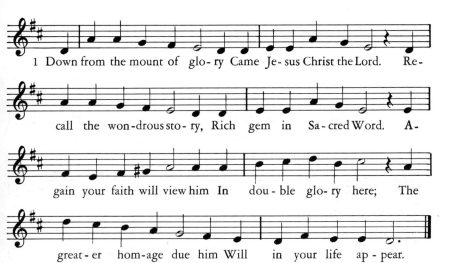

1 Down from the mount of glo-ry Came Je-sus Christ the Lord. Re-
call the won-drous sto-ry, Rich gem in Sa-cred Word. A-
gain your faith will view him In dou-ble glo-ry here; The
great-er hom-age due him Will in your life ap-pear.

2 Transfigured, Christ, the lowly,
Stood radiant in light,
Light found in Godhead solely,
For human eyes too bright.
Then came a voice from heaven,
Confirmed what here we see;
The words "My Son" were given
To seal his deity.

3 Yet mark this glory hidden!
See him the mount descend,
And, by the Father bidden,
His willing footsteps bend
To seek humiliation
In deepest depths of woe,
To suffer degradation
No mind can probe or know.

4 Strange how his journey ended!
In love that is his fame
Our Lord again ascended
A mount—the hill of shame.
Upon the cross he proffered
Himself to agony;
His holy soul he offered
To set the guilty free.

5 Then hail the double glory
Of Jesus Christ, our Lord,
And let the wondrous story
Full peace and joy afford!
The holy mount acclaims him
The Majesty divine;
Mount Calvary proclaims him
Redeemer—yours and mine.

Text: **Werner H. Franzmann** (1904–), *Northwestern Lutheran*, Feb. 18, 1968
Tune: **Ich freu mich in dem Herren**, Bartholomäus Helder, 1648   7. 6. 7. 6. D

Bless the Lord, all his works, in all places of his
dominion. Bless the Lord, O my soul! Psalm
103:22

My Song Is Love Unknown

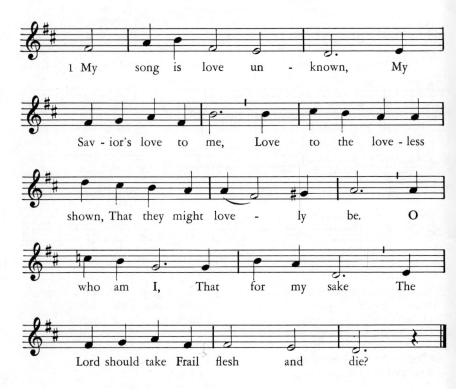

1 My song is love un - known, My
Sav - ior's love to me, Love to the love - less
shown, That they might love - ly be. O
who am I, That for my sake The
Lord should take Frail flesh and die?

2 He came from his blest throne,
Salvation to bestow;
But men made strange, and none
The longed-for Christ would know.
But O my Friend,
My Friend, indeed,
Who at my need
His life did spend!

3 Sometimes they strew his way
And his sweet praises sing;
Resounding all the day
Hosannas to their King.
Then "Crucify!"
Is all their breath,
And for his death
They thirst and cry.

4 Why, what has my Lord done?
What makes this rage and spite?
He made the lame to run,
He gave the blind their sight.
Sweet injuries!
Yet they at these
Themselves displease
And 'gainst him rise.

5 They rise, and needs will have
My dear Lord made away;
A murderer they save,
The Prince of life they slay.
Yet cheerful he
To suffering goes
That he his foes
From thence might free.

6 Here might I stay and sing,
No story so divine;
Never was love, dear King,
Never was grief like thine!
This is my Friend,
In whose sweet praise
I all my days
Could gladly spend.

Text: Samuel Crossman (c. 1624–83), cento
Tune: **Love Unknown,** John Ireland (1879–1962)   6. 6. 6. 6. 4. 4. 4. 4

Deep Were His Wounds, and Red

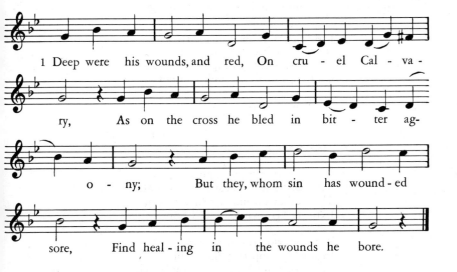

1 Deep were his wounds, and red, On cru - el Cal - va -
ry, As on the cross he bled in bit - ter ag -
o - ny; But they, whom sin has wound - ed
sore, Find heal - ing in the wounds he bore.

2 He suffered shame and scorn,
And wretched, dire disgrace;
Forsaken and forlorn,
He hung there in our place.
But such as would from sin be
   free
Look to his cross for victory.

3 His life, his all, he gave
When he was crucified;
Our burdened souls to save,
What fearful death he died!
But each of us, though dead
   in sin,
Through him eternal life may win.

Text: William Johnson (1906–)
Tune: **Marlee,** Leland Sateren (1913–)   6. 6. 6. 6. 8. 8

The following hymn may also be used:
750 O Love, How Deep, How Broad, How High

727

Ride On, Ride On in Majesty

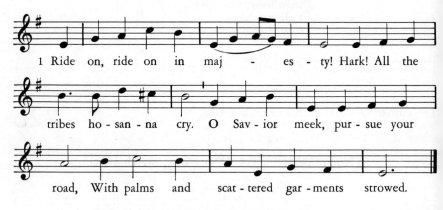

1 Ride on, ride on in maj - es - ty! Hark! All the tribes ho - san - na cry. O Sav - ior meek, pur - sue your road, With palms and scat - tered gar - ments strowed.

2 Ride on, ride on in majesty!
In lowly pomp ride on to die.
O Christ, your triumphs now begin
O'er captive death and conquered sin.

3 Ride on, ride on in majesty!
The angel armies in the sky
Look down with sad and wondering eyes
To see the approaching Sacrifice.

4 Ride on, ride on in majesty!
Your last and fiercest strife is nigh;
The Father on his sapphire throne
Expects his own anointed Son.

5 Ride on, ride on in majesty!
In lowly pomp ride on to die,
Bow your meek head to mortal pain,
Then take, O Christ, your power and reign!

Text: Henry Hart Milman (1791 – 1868), alt.
Tune: The King's Majesty, Graham George, 1940   LM

The steadfast love of the Lord never ceases, his mercies never come to an end; they are new every morning; great is thy faithfulness. Lamentations 3:22-23

Sing, My Tongue, the Glorious Battle

1 Sing, my tongue, the glo-rious bat-tle, Sing the end-ing of the fray;

Now a - bove the cross, the tro- phy, Sound the loud tri - um-phant lay:

Tell how Christ, the world's Re-deem-er As a vic-tim won the day.

2 Tell how, when at length the fullness
   Of the appointed time was come,
   He, the Word, was born of woman,
   Left for us his Father's home,
   Showed to men the perfect manhood,
   Shone as light amidst the gloom.

3 Thus, with thirty years accomplished,
   Went he forth from Nazareth,
   Destined, dedicate, and willing,
   Wrought his work, and met his death;
   Like a lamb he humbly yielded
   On the cross his dying breath.

4 Faithful cross, thou sign of triumph,
   Now for man the noblest tree,
   None in foliage, none in blossom,
   None in fruit thy peer may be;
   Symbol of the world's redemption,
   For the weight that hung on thee!

5 Unto God be praise and glory:
   To the Father and the Son,
   To the eternal Spirit honor
   Now and evermore be done;
   Praise and glory in the highest,
   While the timeless ages run. Amen.

A-men.

Text: Venantius Fortunatus (530−609), cento; trans. John Mason Neale (1818−66), alt.
Tune: **Fortunatus New**, Carl Schalk (*Spirit*, **March 1967**)   8. 7. 8. 7. 8. 7

The Royal Banners Forward Go

(CHORALE)

1 The roy - al ban - ners for-ward go; The cross shines forth in mys - tic glow Where he in flesh, our flesh who made, Our sen - tence bore, our ran - som paid:

2 Where deep for us the spear was dyed,
Life's torrent rushing from his side,
To wash us in that precious flood
Where mingled water flowed and blood.

3 Fulfilled is all that David told
In true prophetic song of old;
Amid the nations, God, said he,
Has reigned and triumphed from the tree.

4 O tree of beauty, tree of light,
O tree with royal purple dight,*
Elect, on whose triumphal breast
Those holy limbs should find their rest;

★ 5 On whose dear arms, so widely flung,
The weight of this world's Ransom hung
The price of humankind to pay
And spoil the Spoiler of his prey.

6 O cross, our one reliance, hail!
So may your power with us avail
To give new virtue to the saint
And pardon to the penitent.

* dight = adorned

7 To thee, eternal Three in One,
Let homage meet by all be done
Whom by the cross thou dost restore,
Preserve, and govern evermore. Amen.

A-men.

Text: Venantius Fortunatus (530–609), cento; sts. 6–7, anonymous; trans. John Mason
Neale (1818–66), alt.

Tunes: **The King's Banner,** ascr. Johann Eccard (1553–1611); **Vexilla regis** (Sarum plainsong, Mode I)
LM

The Christian Year *GOOD FRIDAY*

730

The Royal Banners Forward Go
(PLAINSONG TUNE)

The roy - al ban - - ners for - - ward go;

The cross shines forth in mys - tic glow

Where he in flesh, our flesh who made,

Our sen - - tence bore, our ran - som paid:

7 To thee, eternal Three in One,
Let homage meet by all be done
Whom by the cross thou dost restore,
Preserve, and govern evermore. Amen.

A - men.

Note: For the Vexilla Celebration, the congregation sings the odd-numbered stanzas to the chorale melody,
and the choir sings the even-numbered stanzas to the plainsong melody. The choir Amen is used only when
the choir sings all stanzas.

All Is O'er, the Pain, the Sorrow

1 All is o'er, the pain, the sor - row, Hu - man taunts and
Sa - tan's spite; Death shall be de-spoiled to - mor - row
Of the Prey he grasps to - night. Yet once more, his
own to save, Christ must sleep with - in the grave.

2 Fierce and deadly was the anguish
On the bitter cross he bore;
How did soul and body languish
Till the toil of death was o'er!
But the toil, so fierce and dread,
Bruised and crushed the Serpent's head.

3 Close and still the tomb that holds him
While in brief repose he lies;
Deep the slumber that enfolds him,
Veiled awhile from mortal eyes—
Slumber such as needs must be
After hard-won victory.

4 So this night, with voice of sadness
Chant the anthem soft and low;
Loftier strains of praise and gladness
From tomorrow's harps shall flow:
Death and Hell at length are slain,
Christ has triumphed! Christ does reign!

Text: Gerard Moultrie (1829—85)
Tune: **Psalm 146** (*Genevan Psalter,* 1551)

8. 7. 8. 7. 7. 7

Lord Jesus, Who, Our Souls to Save

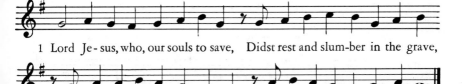

1 Lord Je-sus, who, our souls to save, Didst rest and slum-ber in the grave,

Now grant us all in thee to rest, And here to live as seems thee best.

2 Give us the strength, the dauntless faith
Which thou hast purchased with thy death,
And lead us to that glorious place
Where we shall see the Father's face.

3 O Lamb of God, for sinners slain,
We thank thee for that bitter pain.
Grant that thy death for us may be
Our entrance into life with thee.

Text: Georg Werner (1589–1643); trans. Catherine Winkworth (1829–78), alt.
Tune: **Nun lasst uns den Leib begraben** *(Newe Deudsche Geistliche Gesenge,* Wittenberg, 1544)
LM

Almighty and everlasting God, who hatest
nothing that Thou hast made and dost forgive
the sins of all those who are penitent, create and
make in us new and contrite hearts, that we,
worthily lamenting our sins and acknowledging
our wretchedness, may obtain of Thee, the God
of all mercy, perfect remission and forgiveness;
through Jesus Christ, Thy Son, our Lord, who
liveth and reigneth with Thee and the Holy
Spirit, one God, forever and ever. Amen.

733

At the Lamb's High Feast We Sing

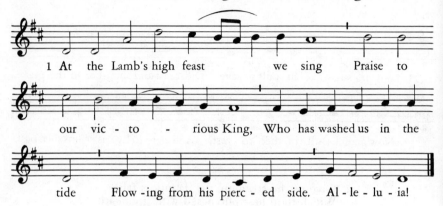

1 At the Lamb's high feast we sing Praise to our vic - to - rious King, Who has washed us in the tide Flow - ing from his pierc - ed side. Al - le - lu - ia!

2 Praise we him, whose love divine
Gives his sacred blood for wine,
Gives his body for the feast,
Christ the Victim, Christ the Priest.
Alleluia!

3 Mighty Victim from the sky,
Hell's fierce powers beneath thee lie;
Thou hast conquered in the fight,
Thou hast brought us life and light.
Alleluia!

4 Now no more can death appall,
Now no more the grave enthrall;
Thou hast opened Paradise,
And in thee thy saints shall rise.
Alleluia!

5 Easter triumph, Easter joy,
Sin alone can this destroy;
From sin's power do thou set free
Souls newborn, O Lord, in thee.
Alleluia!

6 Hymns of glory, songs of praise,
Father, unto thee we raise:
Risen Lord, all praise to thee
With the Spirit ever be.
Alleluia! Amen.

A-men.

Text: 17th-century Office hymn; trans. Robert Campbell (1814—68), cento, alt.
Tune: **Sonne der Gerechtigkeit** (15th-century tune; Bohemian Brethren, 1566) 7. 7. 7. 7. 4

With High Delight Let Us Unite

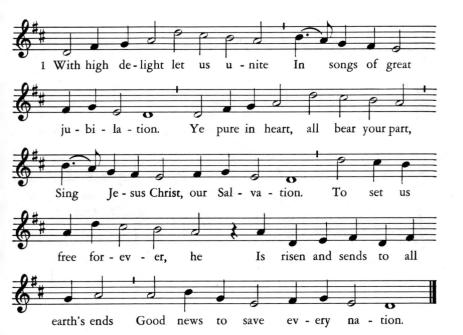

1 With high de-light let us u-nite In songs of great ju-bi-la-tion. Ye pure in heart, all bear your part, Sing Je-sus Christ, our Sal-va-tion. To set us free for-ev-er, he Is risen and sends to all earth's ends Good news to save ev-ery na-tion.

2 True God, he first from death has burst
Forth into life, all subduing.
His Enemy vanquished doth lie;
His death has been death's undoing.
"And yours shall be like victory
O'er death and grave," saith he, who gave
His life for us, life renewing.

3 Let praises ring; give thanks, and bring
To Christ our Lord adoration.
His honor speed by word and deed
To every land, every nation.
So shall his love give us above,
From misery and death set free,
All joy and full consolation.

Text: Georg Vetter (1536–99); trans. Martin H. Franzmann (1907–)
Tune: **Mit Freuden zart** (*Kirchengeseng,* Bohemian Brethren, 1566)   8. 8. 8. 8. 8. 8. 8

O Sons and Daughters of the King

Al - le - lu - ia! Al - le - lu - ia! Al - le - lu - ia!

1 O sons and daugh - ters of the King, Whom heaven - ly

hosts in glo - ry sing, To - day the grave has lost its

After stanza 9

sting. Al - le - lu - ia! Al - le - lu -

ia! Al - le - lu - ia! Al - le - lu - ia!

2 That Easter morn, at break of day,
  The faithful women went their way
  To seek the tomb where Jesus lay.   Alleluia!

3 An angel clad in white they see,
  Who sat and spoke unto the three,
  "Your Lord is gone to Galilee." Alleluia!

4 That night the apostles met in fear;
  Amidst them came their Lord most dear
  And said, "Peace be unto you here."   Alleluia!

5 When Thomas afterwards had heard
  That Jesus had fulfilled his word,
  He doubted if it were the Lord.   Alleluia!

6 "Thomas, behold my side," said he,
  "My hands, my feet, my body see,
  And doubt not, but believe in me."   Alleluia!

7 No longer Thomas then denied;
　He saw the hands, the feet, the side;
　"You are my Lord and God," he cried. Alleluia!

8 Blessèd are they that have not seen
　And yet whose faith has constant been;
　In life eternal they shall reign.   Alleluia!

9 On this most holy day of days,
　To God your hearts and voices raise
　In laud and jubilee and praise.
　　Alleluia! Alleluia! Alleluia!　Alleluia!

Text: 16th-century Latin carol; trans. John Mason Neale (1818 – 66), alt.
Tune: **O filii et filiae** (15th-century French tune, Mode II)　　8. 8. 8 with alleluias

Good Christian Men, Rejoice and Sing

1 Good Chris - tian　men,　re - joice and　sing!　Now　is　the
tri - umph of　our　King!　To　all　the　world glad news we
bring:　Al - le - lu - ia!　Al - le - lu - ia!　Al - le - lu - ia!

2 The Lord of life is risen for aye;
　Bring flowers of song to strew His way;
　Let all mankind rejoice and say:
　Alleluia!

3 Praise we in songs of victory
　That Love, that Life which cannot die,
　And sing with hearts uplifted high:
　Alleluia!

4 Thy name we bless, O risen Lord,
　And sing today with one accord
　The life laid down, the Life restored:
　Alleluia!

Text: Cyril Argentine Alington (1872 – 1955)
Tune: **Gelobt sei Gott**, Melchior Vulpius (c. 1570 – 1615)　　8. 8. 8 with alleluias

That Easter Day with Joy Was Bright

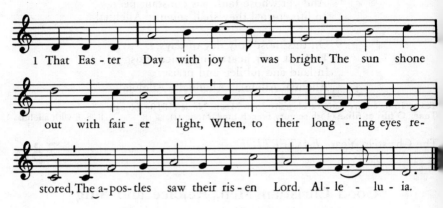

1 That Eas-ter Day with joy was bright, The sun shone
out with fair-er light, When, to their long-ing eyes restored, The a-pos-tles saw their ris-en Lord. Al-le-lu-ia.

2 His risen flesh with radiance glowed;
His wounded hands and feet he showed;
Those scars their solemn witness gave
That Christ was risen from the grave.
Alleluia!

3 O Jesus, King of gentleness,
Do thou thyself our hearts possess
That we may give thee all our days
The willing tribute of our praise.
Alleluia!

4 O Lord of all, with us abide
In this our joyful Eastertide;
From every weapon death can wield
Thine own redeemed forever shield.
Alleluia!

5 All praise, O risen Lord, we give
To thee, who, dead, again dost live;
To God the Father equal praise,
And God the Holy Ghost, we raise.
Alleluia! Amen.

A-men.

Text: Latin, 5th century, cento; trans. *Hymnal 1940* version, based on John Mason Neale
Tune: **Erschienen ist der herrlich Tag**, Nikolaus Herman, (c. 1480 – 1561) LM with alleluia

**Thanks be to God, who gives us the victory
through our Lord Jesus Christ. 1 Corinthians 15:57**

Come, Ye Faithful, Raise the Strain

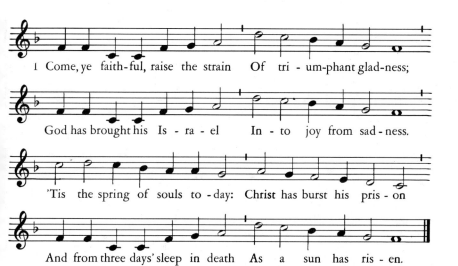

1 Come, ye faith-ful, raise the strain Of tri - um-phant glad-ness;

God has brought his Is - ra - el In - to joy from sad - ness.

'Tis the spring of souls to - day: Christ has burst his pris - on

And from three days' sleep in death As a sun has ris - en.

2 All the winter of our sins,
  Long and dark, is flying
  From his light, to whom we give
  Laud and praise undying.
  Neither could the gates
      of death
  Nor the tomb's dark portal
  Nor the watchers nor the seal
  Hold thee as a mortal.

3 But today amidst thine own
  Thou didst stand, bestowing
  That, thy peace, which evermore
  Passes human knowing.
  Come, ye faithful, raise
      the strain
  Of triumphant gladness;
  God has brought his Israel
  Into joy from sadness.

4 "Alleluia!" now we cry
  To our King immortal,
  Who, triumphant, burst the bars
  Of the tomb's dark portal;
  "Alleluia!" with the Son
  God the Father praising;
  "Alleluia!" yet again
  To the Spirit raising. Amen.

A-men.

Text: John of Damascus (c. 696 – c. 754), cento; trans. John Mason Neale (1818 – 66), abr., alt.
Tune: **Gaudeamus pariter**, Johann Horn (c. 1490 – 1547)   7. 6. 7. 6. D

739

The Day of Resurrection

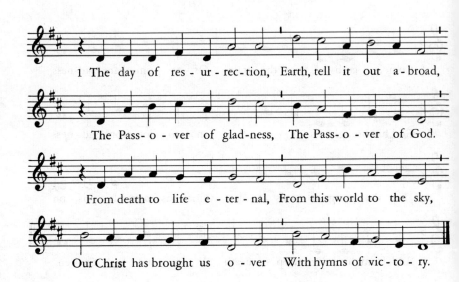

1 The day of res-ur-rec-tion, Earth, tell it out a-broad,
The Pass-o-ver of glad-ness, The Pass-o-ver of God.
From death to life e-ter-nal, From this world to the sky,
Our Christ has brought us o-ver With hymns of vic-to-ry.

2 Our hearts be pure from evil
That we may see aright
The Lord in rays eternal
Of resurrection light
And, listening to his accents,
May hear, so calm and plain,
His own "All hail!" and, hearing,
May raise the victor strain.

3 Now let the heavens be joyful,
Let earth her song begin,
Let all the world keep triumph
And all that is therein.
Let all things, seen and unseen,
Their notes of gladness blend;
For Christ the Lord has risen —
Our Joy that has no end.

4 Then praise we God the Father,
And praise we Christ his Son,
With them the Holy Spirit,
Eternal Three in One,
Till all the ransomed number
Fall down before the throne,
And honor, power, and glory
Ascribe to God alone. Amen.

A-men.

Text: John of Damascus (c. 696 – c. 754); trans. John Mason Neale (1818 – 66), alt.
Tune: **Herzlich tut mich erfreuen** (16th-century tune; Johann Walther recast, 1552)
7. 6. 7. 6. D

The Strife Is O'er, the Battle Done

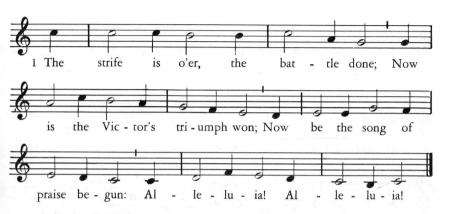

1 The strife is o'er, the bat - tle done; Now
is the Vic - tor's tri - umph won; Now be the song of
praise be - gun: Al - le - lu - ia! Al - le - lu - ia!

2 Death's mightiest powers have done their worst,
And Jesus has his foes dispersed;
Let shouts of praise and joy outburst:
Alleluia! Alleluia!

3 On the third morn he rose again
Glorious in majesty to reign;
O let us swell the joyful strain:
Alleluia! Alleluia!

4 He closed the yawning gates of hell;
The bars from heaven's high portals fell;
Let hymns of praise his triumph tell:
Alleluia! Alleluia!

5 Lord, by the stripes that wounded thee
From death's dread sting thy servants free
That we may live and sing to thee:
Alleluia! Alleluia!

6 In this our Easter joy we raise
To Triune God our song of praise,
Who shows to us his saving ways:
Alleluia! Alleluia! Amen.

A-men.

Text: Anonymous, 1695; trans. Francis Pott (1832 – 1909), alt.
Tune: **Erstanden ist der heilig Christ** (14th-century tune; Bohemian Brethren, 1531)
8. 8. 8 with alleluias

The Victimae Paschali Celebration

Choir

1. Chris-tians, to the Pas-chal Vic-tim Of-fer your thank-ful prais-es!

2. A Lamb the sheep re-deem-eth: Christ who on-ly is sin-less,

Re-con-cil-eth sin-ners to the Fa-ther. Death and life have con-

3. tend-ed In that com-bat stu-pend-ous: The Prince of life, who

died, reigns im-mor-tal.

Congregation

Christ is a-ris-en From the pangs, the pris-on. So let our

joy rise full and free, Christ our Com-fort true will be, Ky-ri-e-leis.
(Lord, have mer-cy.)

Choir

4. Speak, Ma-ry, de-clar-ing What thou saw-est way-far-ing. 5. "The tomb

of Christ, who is liv - ing, The glo-ry of Je-sus' res - ur - rec - tion;

6. Bright an-gels at- test-ing, The shroud and nap-kin rest - ing. Yea, Christ,

7. my Hope, is a - ris - en: To Gal - i - lee he goes be-fore you."

Congregation

Were he not a - ris - en, Then death were still our pris - on. Now,

with him to life re-stored, We praise the Fa-ther of Christ our Lord.

Ky - ri - e - leis.
(Lord, have mer - cy.)

8. Choir

Christ in - deed from death is ris - en, Our new life ob - tain - ing.

Have mer - cy, Vic - tor King, ev - er reign - ing!

Congregation

Al - le - lu - ia! Al - le - lu - ia! Al - le - lu - ia!

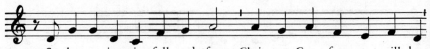

So let our joy rise full and free, Christ our Com-fort true will be.

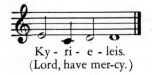

Ky - ri - e - leis.
(Lord, have mer-cy.)

Texts: Sequence ascr. Wipo, 11th century; trans. comp. Anonymous German hymn, c. 1100, trans. Martin L. Seltz (1909—67)

Tunes: **Victimae paschali laudes** (Plainsong, Mode I); **Christ ist erstanden** (12th-century tune; Wittenberg, 1533)

Note: The choir stanzas and the congregation stanzas may be used as two separate hymns.

Now if Christ is preached as raised from the dead, how can some of you say that there is no resurrection of the dead? But if there is no resurrection of the dead, then Christ has not been raised; if Christ has not been raised, then our preaching is in vain and your faith is in vain. We are even found to be misrepresenting God, because we testified of God that he raised Christ, whom he did not raise if it is true that the dead are not raised. For if the dead are not raised, then Christ has not been raised. If Christ has not been raised, your faith is futile and you are still in your sins. Then those also who have fallen asleep in Christ have perished. If for this life only we have hoped in Christ, we are of all men most to be pitied. But in fact Christ has been raised from the dead, the first fruits of those who have fallen asleep. For as by a man came death, by a man has come also the resurrection of the dead. For as in Adam all die, so also in Christ shall all be made alive. 1 Corinthians 15:12-22

This Joyful Eastertide

1 This joy-ful Eas-ter-tide, A-way with sin and sor - - row! My love, the Cru - ci -fied, Has sprung to life this mor - - row: Had Christ, who once was slain, Not burst his three-day pri - son, Our faith had been in vain: But now has Christ a - ris - en, a - ris - en, a - ris - en; But now has Christ a - ris - - en!

2 Death's flood has lost its chill
Since Jesus crossed the river:
Lover of souls, from ill
My passing soul deliver:

3 My flesh in hope shall rest,
And for a season slumber:
Till trump from east to west
Shall wake the dead in number:

Text: George R. Woodward (1848 – 1934)
Tune: **Vruechten** (17th-century Dutch tune)

6. 7. 6. 7 with refrain

743

At the Name of Jesus

1 At the name of Je - sus Ev - ery knee shall bow,

Ev - ery tongue con - fess him King of glo - ry now;

'Tis the Fa - ther's plea - sure We should call him Lord,

Who from the be - gin - ning Was the might - y Word.

2 Humbled for a season
To receive a name
From the lips of sinners
Unto whom he came,
Faithfully he bore it,
Spotless to the last,
Brought it back victorious
When through death he passed.

3 Bore it up triumphant
With its human light,
Through all ranks of creatures,
To the central height,
To the throne of Godhead,
To the Father's breast;
Filled it with the glory
Of that perfect rest.

4 Name him, brothers, name him—
Strong your love as death—
But with awe and wonder,
And with bated breath;
He is God the Savior,
He is Christ the Lord,
Ever to be worshiped,
Evermore adored.

★ 5 In your hearts enthrone him;
There let him subdue
All that is not holy,
All that is not true:
Crown him as your Captain
In temptation's hour;
Let his will enfold you
In its light and power.

★ 6 Brothers, this Lord Jesus
Dwells with us again,
In his Father's wisdom
O'er the earth to reign;
For all wreaths of empire
Meet upon his brow,
And our hearts confess him
King of glory now.

7 Glory then to Jesus,
Who, the Prince of light,
To a world in darkness
Brought the gift of sight;
Praise to God the Father;
In the Spirit's love
Praise we all together
Him who reigns above. Amen.

A-men.

Text: Caroline Maria Noel (1817 — 77), cento, alt.
Tune: **King's Weston**, Ralph Vaughan Williams (1872 — 1958)

6. 5. 6. 5. D

God has gone up with a shout, the Lord with the sound of a trumpet. Psalms 47:5

"Men of Galilee, why do you stand looking into heaven? This Jesus, who was taken up from you into heaven, will come in the same way as you saw him go into heaven." Acts 1:11

See God to Heaven Ascending

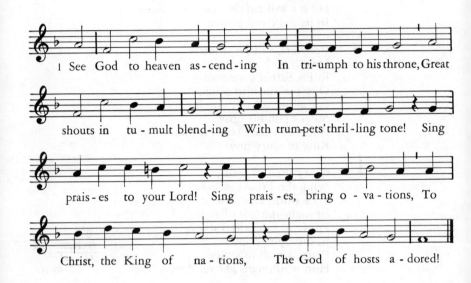

1 See God to heaven as-cend-ing In tri-umph to his throne, Great shouts in tu-mult blend-ing With trum-pets' thril-ling tone! Sing prais-es to your Lord! Sing prais-es, bring o-va-tions, To Christ, the King of na-tions, The God of hosts a-dored!

2 Lo, heaven with joy is sounding
His glad return to see;
Behold the saints surrounding
The Lord who set them free;
Now myriad angels come,
The cherub band rejoices,
And clearest seraph voices
All welcome Jesus home.

3 We see the steps ascending
That raised our Head on high;
We see the highway wending
To heaven's unending joy.
Our Savior leads the way;
Yet he would not bereave us,
A well-marked path would leave us,
Prepares our passageway.

★4 Our minds are heavenward tending,
Where he prepares our place;
Our course on earth is ending,
There to adore his grace.
Bestir your heart and soul!
Where Jesus Christ has entered,
There let your hope be centered;
There run to reach your goal!

5 Let all our thoughts be winging,
With thee to heaven ascend;
Let all our hearts be singing:
"We seek thee, Savior, Friend,
Thee, God's anointed Son,
Our Life and Way to heaven,
To whom all power is given,
Our Joy and Hope and Crown."

Text: Gottfried W. Sacer (1635 – 99), cento; trans. Martin L. Seltz (1909 – 67)
Tune: **Zeuch ein zu deinen Toren,** Johann Crüger (1598 – 1662)   7. 6. 7. 6. 6. 7. 7. 6

Lord God, Thy Praise We Sing

(TE DEUM)

Lord God, thy praise we sing,

Lord God, our thanks we bring.

Fa - ther in e - ter - ni - ty,

All the world hon - ors thee.

All an - gels and hosts a - dore

And wor - ship for - ev - er more.

All cher - u - bim and ser - a - phim

Sing loud, ex - ult with glo - rious hymn:

Ho - ly is God, our Lord!

Ho - ly is God, our Lord!

All

Ho - ly is God, our Lord,

The Lord, the Lord of hosts!

I

Thy maj - es - ty and sov - ereign might
The twelve a - pos - tles praise thee all;
Vic - to - rious, no - ble mar - tyrs raise
All Chris- ten - dom on earth to thee
Thee, Fa - ther on thy high - est throne,
The Ho - ly Ghost, our Par - a - clete,

II

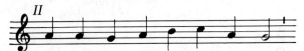

Fill all the earth and realms of light.
The proph - ets old thy name ex - tol.
Their voice to thee in songs of praise.
Sings hymns of praise un - ceas - ing - ly.
Thy true and sole - be - got - ten Son,
The Church ex - alts in ser - vice meet.

I

Christ, King of glo - ry, thee we own,
To save us, wretch-ed and for - lorn,
Thou o - ver - cam - est death's sharp sting
At God's right hand ex - alt - ed, thou
Thou wilt re - turn, clothed in thy might,

II

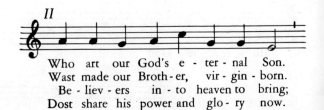

Who art our God's e - ter - nal Son.
Wast made our Broth - er, vir - gin - born.
Be - liev - ers in - to heaven to bring;
Dost share his power and glo - ry now.
To judge the quick and dead a - right.

Help us, thy ser-vants, now, O God,

Whom thou hast ran-somed with ho - ly blood.

O Lord, with all thy saints may we

In - her - it heaven and dwell with thee.

Help us, O Lord, from age to age,

And bless thy chos - en her - i - tage.

Nour-ish and keep them by thy power,

And lift them up for - ev - er - more.

Dai - ly our thanks we sing to thee,

Re - vere thy name e - ter - nal - ly.

A - - men.

Text: Martin Luther (1483 – 1546), cento; trans. Walter E. Buszin (1899 –)
Tune: **Te Deum**, Martin Luther, 1529 (Based on a plainsong tune)

I Bind unto Myself Today

I bind un-to my-self to-day The
strong name of the Trin-i-ty, By in-vo-
ca-tion of the same, The Three in
One and One in Three. 1 I bind this
day to me for-ev-er, By power of
faith, Christ's in-car-na-tion; His bap-tism
in the Jor-dan riv-er; His death on
cross for my sal-va-tion; His burst-ing
from the spi-ced tomb; His rid-ing
up the heaven-ly way; His com-ing

at the day of doom; I bind un - to my - self to - day.

* *Stanzas 1, 2, 3, 4 begin here.*

★ 2 I bind unto myself today
     The virtues of the starlit heaven,
     The glorious sun's life-giving ray,
     The whiteness of the moon at even,
     The flashing of the lightning free,
     The whirling wind's tempestuous shocks,
     The stable earth, the deep salt sea,
     Around the old eternal rocks.

  3 I bind unto myself today
     The power of God to hold and lead,
     His eye to watch, his might to stay,
     His ear to hearken to my need,
     The wisdom of my God to teach,
     His hand to guide, his shield to ward,
     The word of God to give me speech,
     His heavenly host to be my guard.

  4 I bind unto myself the name,
     The strong name of the Trinity;
     By invocation of the same,
     The Three in One and One in Three —
     Of whom all nature has creation —
     Eternal Father, Spirit, Word:
     Praise to the Lord of my salvation,
     Salvation is of Christ the Lord. Amen.

A-men.

Text: Ascr. St. Patrick (c. 372 – 466), cento; paraphr. Cecil Frances Alexander (1823 – 95)
Tune: **St. Patrick's Breastplate** (Traditional Irish tune)   **LMD**

747

Thy Strong Word Did Cleave the Darkness

1 Thy strong word did cleave the dark - ness;
At thy speak - ing it was done; For cre - at - ed
light we thank thee, While thine or - dered sea - sons run:
Al - le - lu - ia! Al - le - lu - ia! Praise to thee, who
light dost send! Al - le - lu - ia! Al - le - lu - ia!
Al - le - lu - ia with - out end!

2 Lo, on men who dwelt in darkness,
Dark as night and deep as death,
Broke the light of thy salvation,
Breathed thine own life-breathing breath:
Alleluia! Alleluia!
Praise to thee who light dost send!
Alleluia! Alleluia!
Alleluia without end!

3 Thy strong word bespeaks us righteous;
Bright with thine own holiness,
Glorious now, we press toward glory,
And our lives our hopes confess:
Alleluia! Alleluia!
Praise to thee who light dost send!
Alleluia! Alleluia!
Alleluia without end!

4 From the cross thy wisdom shining
  Breaketh forth in conquering might;
  From the cross forever beameth
  All thy bright redeeming light:
  Alleluia! Alleluia!
  Praise to thee who light dost send!
  Alleluia! Alleluia!
  Alleluia without end!

5 Give us lips to sing thy glory,
  Tongues thy mercy to proclaim,
  Throats that shout the hope that fills us,
  Mouths to speak thy holy name:
  Alleluia! Alleluia!
  May the light which thou dost send
  Fill our songs with alleluias,
  Alleluias without end!

6 God the Father, Light-Creator,
  To thee laud and honor be;
  To thee, Light of Light begotten,
  Praise be sung eternally;
  Holy Spirit, Light-Revealer,
  Glory, glory be to thee;
  Men and angels, now and ever
  Praise the Holy Trinity. Amen.

A-men.

Text: Martin H. Franzmann (1907 –)
Tune: **Ebenezer**, Thomas John Williams (1869 – 1944)

8. 7. 8. 7. D

O Lord, our heavenly Father, almighty and ever-lasting God, who hast safely brought us to the beginning of this day, defend us in the same with Thy mighty power and grant that this day we fall into no sin, neither run into any kind of danger, but that all our doings, being ordered by Thy governance, may be righteous in Thy sight; through Jesus Christ, Thy Son, our Lord, who liveth and reigneth with Thee and the Holy Spirit, one God, forever and ever. Amen.

Eternal God, Whose Power Upholds

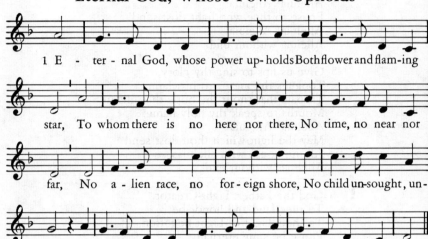

1 E - ter - nal God, whose power up- holds Both flower and flam-ing
star, To whom there is no here nor there, No time, no near nor
far, No a - lien race, no for - eign shore, No child un-sought, unknown, O send us forth as proph- ets true, To make all lands thine own!

2 O God of truth, which science seeks,
Whom reverent souls adore,
Who lightest every earnest mind
Of every clime and shore,
Dispel the gloom of error's night,
Of ignorance and fear,
Until true wisdom from above
Shall make life's pathway clear!

3 O God of beauty, oft revealed
In dreams of human art,
In speech that flows to melody,
In holiness of heart,
Teach us to ban all ugliness
That blinds our eyes to thee,
Till all shall know the loveliness
Of lives made fair and free.

4 O God of righteousness and grace,
Seen in the Christ, thy Son,
Whose life and death reveal thy face,
By whom thy will was done,
Inspire thy heralds of good news
To live thy life divine,
Till Christ is formed in all mankind
And every land is thine!

Text: Henry Hallam Tweedy (1868–1953), alt.
Tune: **Pilgrim** (*Southern Harmony*, 1835)

CMD

Hope of the World

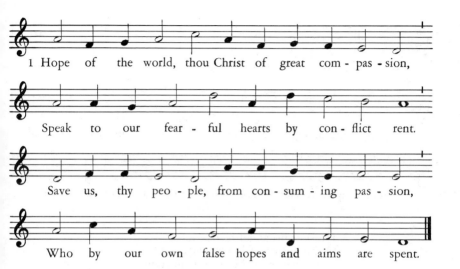

1 Hope of the world, thou Christ of great com-pas-sion,
Speak to our fear-ful hearts by con-flict rent.
Save us, thy peo-ple, from con-sum-ing pas-sion,
Who by our own false hopes and aims are spent.

2 Hope of the world, God's gift from highest heaven,
Bringing to hungry souls the bread of life,
Still let thy spirit unto us be given
To heal earth's wounds and end her bitter strife.

3 Hope of the world, afoot on dusty highways,
Showing to wandering souls the path of light,
Walk thou beside us lest the tempting byways
Lure us away from thee to endless night.

4 Hope of the world, who by thy cross didst save us
From death and dark despair, from sin and guilt,
We render back the love thy mercy gave us;
Take thou our lives and use them as thou wilt.

5 Hope of the world, O Christ, o'er death victorious,
Who by this sign didst conquer grief and pain,
We would be faithful to thy Gospel glorious:
Thou art our Lord! Thou dost forever reign!

Text: Georgia Harkness (1891 –)
Tune: **Donne secours** (Psalm 12 in *Genevan Psalter*, 1551) 11. 10. 11. 10

750

O Love, How Deep, How Broad, How High

1 O Love, how deep, how broad, how high,
How passing thought and fantasy,
That God, the Son of God, should take
Our mortal form for mortals' sake!

2 He sent no angel to our race
Of higher or of lower place,
But wore the robe of human frame,
And he himself to this world came.

3 Nor willed he only to appear,
His pleasure was to tarry here;
And God and Man with man would be
The space of thirty years and three.

4 For us baptized, for us he bore
His holy fast and hungered sore;
For us temptation sharp he knew,
For us the Tempter overthrew.

5 For us he prayed, for us he taught,
For us his daily works he wrought,
By words and signs and actions thus
Still seeking not himself, but us.

6 For us to wicked men betrayed,
Scourged, mocked, in crown of thorns arrayed;
He bore the shameful cross and death,
For us he gave his dying breath.

7 For us he rose from death again,
For us he went on high to reign;
For us he sent his Spirit here,
To guide, to strengthen, and to cheer.

8 In this great triumph of our King
To God on high all praise we bring,
To him all thanks and laud give we,
The ever-blessèd Trinity. Amen.

A-men.

Text: Ascr. Thomas à Kempis (1380–1471), cento; trans. Benjamin Webb (1820–85), alt.
Tune: **Deo gracias** (Traditional English tune, 15th century)   LM

The Trinity *THE REDEEMER*

Hymn of the Week, Trinity XII

751

O Thou Who Once in Galilee

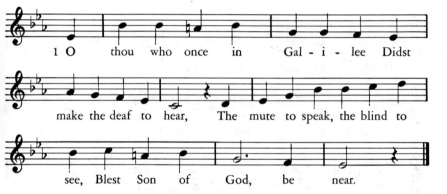

1 O thou who once in Galilee Didst make the deaf to hear, The mute to speak, the blind to see, Blest Son of God, be near.

2 O deign to hear the silent prayer
Of thine afflicted own;
Yea, bid them cast on thee all care,
Thy grace to them make known.

3 The speechless tongue, the lifeless ear
Thou canst restore, O Lord;
Thine "Ephphatha," O Savior dear,
Can instant help afford.

4 Meanwhile in them the listening ear
Of faith in thee impart,
And let thy Word bring light and cheer
To every troubled heart.

5 Then in thy heaven's happy land
Each loss will prove a gain;
All mysteries we'll understand
For thou wilt make them plain.

Text: Anna Hoppe (1889–1941)
Tune: **Salem**, Richard Hillert (1923–)   CM

752

Son of God, Eternal Savior

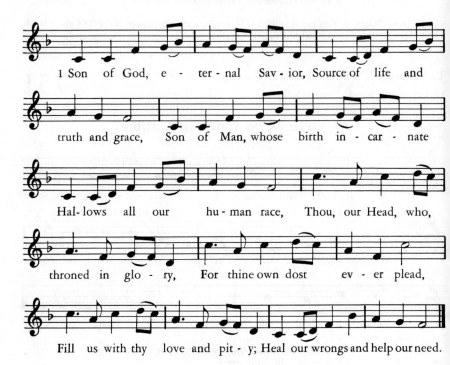

1 Son of God, e - ter - nal Sav - ior, Source of life and
truth and grace, Son of Man, whose birth in - car - nate
Hal - lows all our hu - man race, Thou, our Head, who,
throned in glo - ry, For thine own dost ev - er plead,
Fill us with thy love and pit - y; Heal our wrongs and help our need.

2 Bind us all as one together
In thy Church's sacred fold,
Weak and healthy, poor and wealthy,
Sad and joyful, young and old.
Is there want or pain or sorrow?
Make us all the burden share.
Are there spirits crushed and broken?
Teach us, Lord, to soothe their care.

3 As thou, Lord, hast lived for others,
So may we for others live;
Freely have thy gifts been granted,
Freely may thy servants give —
Thine the gold and thine the silver,
Thine the wealth of land and sea,
We but stewards of thy bounty
Held in solemn trust for thee.

4 Come, O Christ, and reign among us,
  King of love and Prince of peace,
  Hush the storm of strife and passion,
  Bid its cruel discords cease;
  By thy patient years of toiling,
  By thy silent hours of pain,
  Quench our fevered thirst of pleasure,
  Shame our selfish greed of gain.

5 Son of God, eternal Savior,
  Source of life and truth and grace,
  Son of Man, whose birth incarnate
  Hallows all our human race,
  By thy praying, by thy willing
  That thy people should be one,
  Grant, O grant our hope's fruition:
  Here on earth thy will be done.

Text: Somerset C. Lowry (1855–1932), cento
Tune: **Lord, Revive Us** (Early American tune)   8. 7. 8. 7. D

The following hymn may also be used:
743 **At the Name of Jesus**

"Let not your hearts be troubled; believe in God, believe also in me. In my Father's house are many rooms; if it were not so, would I have told you that I go to prepare a place for you? And when I go and prepare a place for you, I will come again and will take you to myself, that where I am you may be also. And you know the way where I am going." Thomas said to him, "Lord, we do not know where you are going; how can we know the way?" Jesus said to him, "I am the way, and the truth, and the life; no one comes to the Father, but by me. If you had known me, you would have known my Father also; henceforth you know him and have seen him."

Philip said to him, "Lord, show us the Father, and we shall be satisfied." Jesus said to him, "Have I been with you so long, and yet you do not know me, Philip? He who has seen me has seen the Father; how can you say, 'Show us the Father'?" John 14:1-9

Now Let Us Pray to God the Holy Ghost

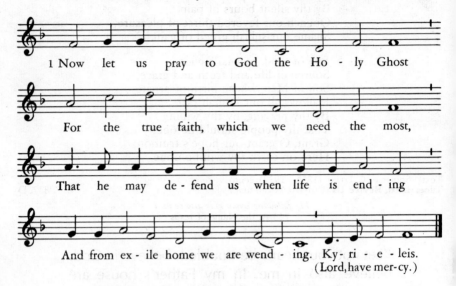

1 Now let us pray to God the Ho- ly Ghost

For the true faith, which we need the most,

That he may de- fend us when life is end- ing

And from ex- ile home we are wend- ing. Ky- ri- e - leis.
(Lord, have mer- cy.)

2 Shine in our hearts, O thou most precious Light,
Teach us Jesus Christ to know aright,
That we may abide in the Lord who bought us;
To our homeland true he has brought us.
Kyrieleis. [Lord, have mercy.]

3 Thou sacred Love, thy grace on us bestow,
Set our hearts with heavenly fire aglow
That with hearts united we love each other,
Of one mind, in peace with our brother.
Kyrieleis. [Lord, have mercy.]

4 Thou highest Comfort in our every need,
Help us neither scorn nor death to heed,
That we may not falter nor courage fail us
When the Foe shall rail and assail us.
Kyrieleis. [Lord, have mercy.]

Text: St. 1, author unknown, c. 1250; sts. 2–4, Martin Luther (1483–1546); trans. composite, 1965
Tune: **Nun bitten wir** (13th-century German tune)   10. 9. 11. 9. 4

Eager to maintain the unity of the Spirit in the bond of peace. Ephesians 4:3

Holy Spirit, Ever Dwelling

1 Holy Spirit, ever dwelling In the holiest realms of light;

Holy Spirit, ever brooding O'er a world of gloom and night;

Holy Spirit, ever raising Sons of earth to thrones on high;

Living life-imparting Spirit, Thee we praise and magnify.

2 Holy Spirit, ever living
  As the Church's very life;
  Holy Spirit, ever striving
  Through her in a ceaseless strife;
  Holy Spirit, ever forming
  In the Church the mind of Christ;
  Thee we praise with endless worship
  For thy fruit and gifts unpriced.

3 Holy Spirit, ever working
  Through the Church's ministry;
  Quickening, strengthening, and absolving,
  Setting captive sinners free;
  Holy Spirit, ever binding
  Age to age and soul to soul,
  In a fellowship unending
  Thee we worship and extol.

Text: Timothy Rees (1874 – 1939)
Tune: **In Babilone** (Traditional Dutch tune)   8. 7. 8. 7. D

Come Down, O Love Divine

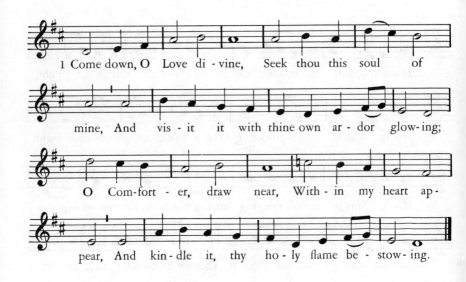

1 Come down, O Love di-vine, Seek thou this soul of
mine, And vis-it it with thine own ar-dor glow-ing;
O Com-fort-er, draw near, With-in my heart ap-
pear, And kin-dle it, thy ho-ly flame be-stow-ing.

2 O let it freely burn
   Till earthly passions turn
   To dust and ashes in its heat consuming;
   And let thy glorious light
   Shine ever on my sight
   And clothe me round, the while my path illuming.

3 Let holy charity
   Mine outward vesture be
   And lowliness become mine inner clothing—
   True lowliness of heart
   Which takes the humbler part
   And o'er its own shortcomings weeps with loathing.

4 And so the yearning strong
   With which the soul will long
   Shall far outpass the power of human telling;
   For none can guess its grace
   Till he become the place
   Wherein the Holy Spirit makes his dwelling.

Text: Bianco da Siena (d. 1434), cento; paraphr. Richard Frederick Littledale (1833—90)
Tune: **Down Ampney**, Ralph Vaughan Williams (1872—1958)   6. 6. 11. D

From All Thy Saints in Warfare

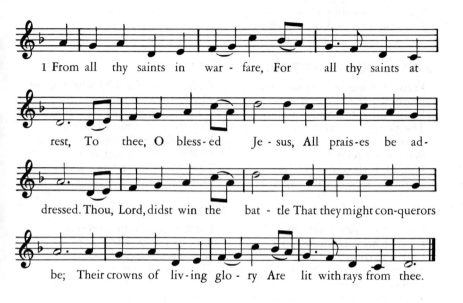

1 From all thy saints in war - fare, For all thy saints at rest, To thee, O bless-ed Je - sus, All prais-es be ad-dressed. Thou, Lord, didst win the bat - tle That they might con-querors be; Their crowns of liv-ing glo - ry Are lit with rays from thee.

2 *(Here insert the stanza for the special day.)*

3 Then praise we God the Father,
  And praise we God the Son
  And God the Holy Spirit,
  Eternal Three in One,
  Till all the ransomed number
  Fall down before the throne
  And honor, power, and glory
  Ascribe to God alone. Amen.

A-men.

GENERAL STANZA (when no specific one is available)
  Apostles, prophets, martyrs,
  And all the sacred throng
  Who wear the spotless raiment,
  Who raise the ceaseless song—
  For these, passed on before us,
  Savior, we thee adore,
  And, walking in their footsteps,
  Would serve thee more and more.

ANDREW

Praise, Lord, for thine apostle,
The first to welcome thee,
The first to lead his brother
The very Christ to see.
With hearts for thee made ready,
May we throughout the year
Still watch to lead our brethren
To own thine advent near.

CONVERSION OF ST. PAUL

Praise for the light from heaven,
Praise for the voice of awe,
Praise for the glorious vision
The persecutor saw.
Thee, Lord, for his conversion
We glorify today;
Enlighten all our darkness
With thy true Spirit's ray.

HOLY INNOCENTS

Praise for thine infant martyrs,
By thee with tenderest love
Called early from the warfare
To share the rest above.
O Rachel, cease your weeping;
They rest from pains and cares.
Lord, grant us hearts as guileless
And crowns as bright as theirs.

JAMES THE ELDER

For him, O Lord, we praise thee,
Who, slain by Herod's sword,
Drank of thy cup of suffering,
Fulfilling thus thy word.
Curb we all vain impatience
To read thy veiled decree,
And count it joy to suffer
If so brought nearer thee.

JOHN THE EVANGELIST

Praise for the loved disciple,
Exile on Patmos' shore;
Praise for the faithful record
He to thy Godhead bore.
Praise for the mystic vision
Through him to us revealed;
May we, in patience waiting,
With thine elect be sealed.

BARTHOLOMEW

All praise for thine apostle,
The faithful, pure and true,
Whom underneath the fig tree
Thine eye all-seeing knew;
Like him may we be guileless —
True Israelites indeed —
That thine abiding presence
Our longing souls may feed.

MATTHEW

Praise, Lord, for him whose Gospel
Thy human life declared,
Who, worldly gains forsaking,
Thy path of suffering shared.
From all unrighteous mammon,
O give us hearts set free
That we, whate'er our calling,
May rise and follow thee.

MATTHIAS THE APOSTLE

Lord, thine abiding presence
Directs the wondrous choice;
For one in place of Judas
The faithful now rejoice.
The Church from false apostles
Forevermore defend,
And by thy parting promise
Be with her to the end.

NATIVITY OF JOHN THE BAPTIST

We praise thee for the Baptist,
Forerunner of the Word,
Our true Elias, making
A highway for the Lord.
Of prophets last and greatest,
He saw thy dawning ray,
Make us the rather blessèd,
Who love thy glorious day.

PETER

Praise for thy great apostle,
The eager and the bold;
Thrice falling, yet repentant,
Thrice charged to feed thy fold.
Lord, make thy pastors faithful
To guard their flocks from ill,
And grant them dauntless courage
With humble earnest will.

LUKE THE EVANGELIST

For that beloved physician
All praise, whose Gospel shows
The Healer of the nations,
The Sharer of our woes.
Thy wine and oil, O Savior,
On bruised hearts deign to pour,
And with true balm of Gilead
Anoint us evermore.

MARK THE EVANGELIST

For him, O Lord, we praise thee,
The weak by grace made strong,
Whose labors and whose Gospel
Enrich our triumph song.
May we in all our weakness
Find strength from thee supplied
And all as fruitful branches
In thee, the Vine, abide.

STEPHEN THE MARTYR

Praise for the first of martyrs,
Who saw thee ready stand
To aid in midst of torment,
To plead at God's right hand.
Share we with him, if summoned
By death our Lord to own,
On earth the faithful witness,
In heaven the martyr-crown.

PHILIP AND JAMES

All praise for thine apostle,
Blest guide to Greek and Jew,
And him surnamed thy brother;
Keep us thy brethren true.
And grant the grace to know thee,
The Way, the Truth, the Life,
To wrestle with temptations
Till victors in the strife.

SIMON AND JUDE

Praise, Lord, for thine apostles
Who sealed their faith today;
One love, one zeal impelled them
To tread the sacred way.
May we with zeal as earnest
The faith of Christ maintain
And, bound in love as brethren,
At length thy rest attain.

THOMAS

All praise for thine apostle,
Whose short-lived doubtings prove
Thy perfect twofold nature,
The fullness of thy love.
On all who wait thy coming
Shed forth thy peace, O Lord,
And grant us faith to know thee,
True Man, true God, adored.

Text: Horatio, Earl Nelson (1823 – 1913) et al.
Tune: **King's Lynn** (Traditional English tune)

7. 6. 7. 6. D

Set your minds on things that are above, not on things that are on earth. For you have died, and your life is hid with Christ in God. When Christ who is our life appears, then you also will appear with him in glory. Colossians 3:2-4

O Kingly Love, That Faithfully

1 O king-ly Love, that faith-ful-ly Didst keep thine

an-cient prom-is-es, Didst bid the bid-den come to thee,

The peo-ple thou didst choose to bless, This day we

raise Our song of praise, A-dor-ing thee,

That in the days When a-lien sound Had all but

drowned Thine an-cient, true, and con-stant mel-o-dy,

Thy might-y hand did make A trum-pet none could

si-lence or mis-take; Thy liv-ing breath did blow for

all the world to hear, Liv-ing and clear: The feast is

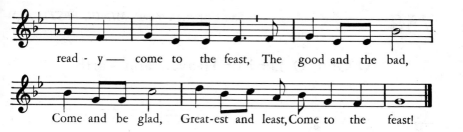

read-y — come to the feast, The good and the bad,
Come and be glad, Great-est and least, Come to the feast!

2 O lavish Love, that didst prepare
A table bounteous as thy heart,
That men might leave their puny care
And taste and see how good thou art,
        This day we raise, *etc.*

3 O seeking Love, thy hurrying feet
Go searching still to urge and call
The bad and good on every street
To fill thy boundless banquet hall.
        This day we raise, *etc.*

4 O holy Love, thou canst not brook
Man's cool and careless enmity;
O ruthless Love, thou wilt not look
On man robed in contempt of thee.
        Thine echoes die;
        Our deeds deny
        Thy summoning:
        Our darkling cry,
        Our meddling sound
        Have all but drowned
        That song that once made every echo ring.
        Take up again, O take
        The trumpet none can silence or mistake,
        And blow once more for us and all the world to hear,
        Living and clear:
        The feast is ready — come to the feast,
        The good and the bad,
        Come and be glad,
        Greatest and least,
        Come to the feast!

Text: Martin H. Franzmann (1907 –)
Tune: **Kingly Love**, Richard Hillert (1923 –)

                                          LM with refrain

O God, O Lord of Heaven and Earth

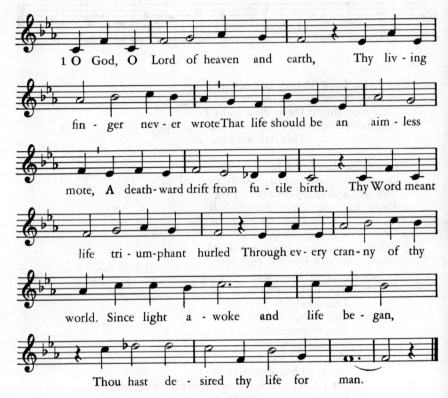

1 O God, O Lord of heaven and earth, Thy liv-ing
fin-ger nev-er wrote That life should be an aim-less
mote, A death-ward drift from fu-tile birth. Thy Word meant
life tri-um-phant hurled Through ev-ery cran-ny of thy
world. Since light a-woke and life be-gan,
Thou hast de-sired thy life for man.

2 Our fatal will to equal thee,
   Our rebel will wrought death and night.
   We seized and used in thy despite
   Thy wondrous gift of liberty.
   We housed us in this house of doom,
   Where death had royal scope and room,
   Until thy Servant, Prince of peace,
   Breached all its walls for our release.

3 Thou camest to our hall of death,
   O Christ, to breathe our poisoned air,
   To drink for us the dark despair
   That strangled man's reluctant breath.
   How beautiful the feet that trod
   The road that leads us back to God.
   How beautiful the feet that ran
   To bring the great good news to man.

A-men.

LMD

The Church *CHRISTIAN UNITY*

759

In Adam We Have All Been One

1 In A - dam we have all been one, One huge re - bel - lious
man; We all have fled that Eve-ning Voice That sought us as we ran.

2 We fled thee, and in losing thee
  We lost our brother too;
  Each singly sought and claimed his own;
  Each man his brother slew.

3 But thy strong love, it sought us still
  And sent thine only Son
  That we might hear his Shepherd's voice
  And, hearing him, be one.

4 O thou who, when we loved thee not,
  Didst love and save us all,
  Thou great Good Shepherd of mankind,
  O hear us when we call.

5 Send us thy Spirit, teach us truth;
  Thou Son, O set us free
  From fancied wisdom, self-sought ways,
  To make us one in thee.

6 Then shall our song united rise
  To thine eternal throne,
  Where with the Father evermore
  And Spirit thou art One. Amen.

A-men.

Text: Martin H. Franzmann (1907 –)
Tune: **The Saints' Delight** (*Southern Harmony*, 1835)

CM

Speak Forth Thy Word, O Father

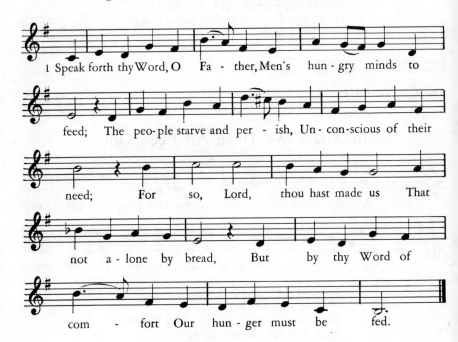

1 Speak forth thy Word, O Father, Men's hungry minds to feed; The people starve and perish, Unconscious of their need; For so, Lord, thou hast made us That not alone by bread, But by thy Word of comfort Our hunger must be fed.

2 The secrets of the atom,
The universe of light,
All wonders of creation
Proclaim thy boundless might:
But only through the witness
From man to man passed on
Dost thou reveal in fullness
The Gospel of thy Son.

3 Take us, then, Lord, and use us
Thy messengers to be:
Our prayers, our gifts, our service
We offer here to thee,
That every man and nation
May learn what we have heard,
And all the minds of millions
Shall feed upon thy Word. Amen.

A-men.

Text: Charles Jeffries, 1967, cento
Tune: **Speak Forth Thy Word**, Theodore A. Beck (1929—)

7. 6. 7. 6. D

The Sending, Lord, Springs from Thy Yearning Heart

1 The send - ing, Lord, springs from thy yearn - ing heart.

God, thou the Send - er, thou the Sent One art, And

of thy mis - sion mak - est us a part.

Al - le - lu - ia! Al - le - lu - ia!

2 Thy body paid for men of every race;
To them we witness, Christ, thy boundless grace,
With them, one body, kneel before thy face.
Alleluia! Alleluia!

3 Where men their brothers heartlessly oppress,
Where people suffer, hopeless in distress,
There we thy name in deed and word confess.
Alleluia! Alleluia!

4 One man in need in body, mind, and soul;
One word in Jesus' name to make him whole;
One Lord, one mission leads us to the goal.
Alleluia! Alleluia!

5 One mission takes me over land and sea
And to the Christian brother next to me.
Help me to listen, Lord, and speak for thee.
Alleluia! Alleluia!

6 From urban deeps to orbits high in space
Through cross to glory moves one pilgrim race,
Praising the Father-Son-and-Spirit's grace;
Alleluia! Alleluia! Amen.

A-men.

Text: William J. Danker (1914—)
Tune: **Mission**, Richard Hillert (1923—)

10. 10. 10 with alleluias

762

Stand, Soldier of the Cross

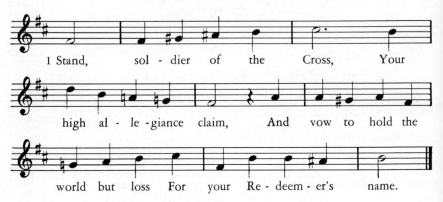

1 Stand, sol - dier of the Cross, Your high al - le -giance claim, And vow to hold the world but loss For your Re - deem - er's name.

2 Arise and be baptized
To wash your sins away;
Your league with God be solemnized,
Your faith confessed today.

3 No more your own, but Christ's,
With all the saints of old,
Apostles, seers, evangelists,
And martyr throngs enrolled.

4 O bright the conqueror's crown,
The song of triumph sweet,
When faith casts every trophy down
At our great Captain's feet.

5 All glory to the Son,
Who comes to set us free,
With Father, Spirit, ever One,
Through all eternity. Amen.

A-men.

Text: Edward Henry Bickersteth (1825 – 1906), cento, alt.
Tune: **Song 20,** Orlando Gibbons (1583 – 1625)   SM

He will not let your foot be moved, he who keeps
you will not slumber. Behold, he who keeps
Israel will neither slumber nor sleep. Psalm
121:3-4

With Christ We Share a Mystic Grave

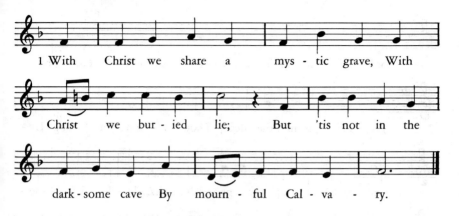

1 With Christ we share a mys - tic grave, With
Christ we bur - ied lie; But 'tis not in the
dark - some cave By mourn - ful Cal - va - ry.

2 The pure and bright baptismal flood
  Entombs our nature's stain:
  New creatures from the cleansing wave
  With Christ we rise again.

3 Thrice blest, if through this world of sin
  And lust and selfish care
  Our resurrection mantle white
  And undefiled we wear.

4 Thrice blest, if through the gates of death,
  At last in glory free,
  We to our joyful rising pass,
  O risen Lord, with thee.

5 And now to thy thrice holy name,
  The God whom we adore,
  To Father, Son, and Holy Ghost,
  Be glory evermore. Amen.

A-men.

Text: John Mason Neale (1818–66)
Tune: **Farrant**, ascr. Richard Farrant (d. 1581)

CM

We were buried therefore with him by baptism
into death, so that as Christ was raised from the
dead by the glory of the Father, we too might
walk in newness of life. Romans 6:4

764

Lord, Enthroned in Heavenly Splendor

1 Lord, en - throned in heaven - ly splen - dor, First - be -
got - ten from the dead, Thou a - lone, our strong De -
fend - er, Lift - est up thy peo-ple's head. Al-le - lu - ia! Al - le -
lu - ia! Al - le - lu - ia! Je - sus, true and liv - ing
Bread! Je - sus true and liv - ing Bread!

2 Here our humblest homage pay we;
Here in loving reverence bow;
Here for faith's discernment pray we,
Lest we fail to know thee now.
Alleluia! Alleluia! Alleluia!
Thou art here, we ask not how.

3 Though the lowliest form doth veil thee
As of old in Bethlehem,
Here as there thine angels hail thee
Branch and Flower of Jesse's stem.
Alleluia! Alleluia! Alleluia!
We in worship join with them.

4 Paschal Lamb, thine offering, finished
Once for all when thou wast slain,
In its fullness undiminished
Shall forevermore remain,
Alleluia! Alleluia! Alleluia!
Cleansing souls from every stain.

5 Life-imparting heavenly Manna,
  Stricken Rock with streaming side,
  Heaven and earth with loud hosanna
  Worship thee, the Lamb who died,
  Alleluia! Alleluia! Alleluia!
  Risen, ascended, glorified!

Text: George H. Bourne (1840–1925)
Tune: **Bryn Calfaria**, William Owen (1814–93)   8. 7. 8. 7. 4. 4. 4. 7. 7

The following hymn may also be used:
733 At the Lamb's High Feast We Sing

The Church *HOLY COMMUNION*   # 765

Here, O My Lord, I See Thee Face to Face

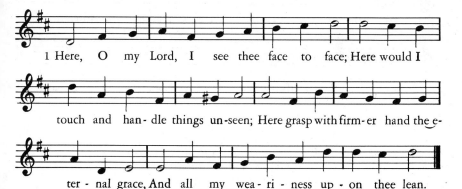

1 Here, O my Lord, I see thee face to face; Here would I
touch and han-dle things un-seen; Here grasp with firm-er hand the e-
ter-nal grace, And all my wea-ri-ness up-on thee lean.

2 Here would I feed upon the bread of God;
  Here drink with thee the royal wine of heaven;
  Here would I lay aside each earthly load,
  Here taste afresh the calm of sin forgiven.

3 Too soon we rise; the vessels disappear;
  The feast, though not the love, is passed and gone.
  The bread and wine remove, but thou art here—
  Nearer than ever—still my Shield and Sun.

4 Feast after feast thus comes and passes by;
  Yet, passing, points to the glad feast above,
  Giving sweet foretaste of the festal joy,
  The Lamb's great bridal feast of bliss and love.

Text: Horatius Bonar (1808–89), cento †
Tune: **Farley Castle**, ascr. Henry Lawes (1596–1662)   10. 10. 10. 10

Let All Mortal Flesh Keep Silence

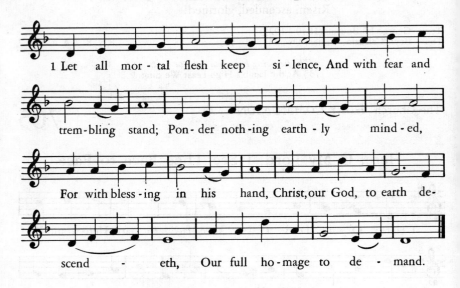

1 Let all mor-tal flesh keep si-lence, And with fear and trem-bling stand; Pon-der noth-ing earth-ly mind-ed, For with bless-ing in his hand, Christ, our God, to earth de-scend - eth, Our full ho-mage to de - mand.

2 King of kings, yet born of Mary,
As of old on earth he stood,
Lord of lords, in human vesture—
In the body and the blood—
He will give to all the faithful
His own Self for heavenly food.

3 Rank on rank the host of heaven
Spreads its vanguard on the way,
As the Light of Light descendeth
From the realms of endless day,
That the powers of hell may vanish
As the darkness clears away.

4 At his feet the six-winged seraph;
Cherubim with sleepless eye
Veil their faces to the Presence,
As with ceaseless voice they cry:
Alleluia! Alleluia!
Alleluia, Lord most high!

Text: Gerard Moultrie (1829—85)
Tune: **Picardy** (Traditional French carol)   8. 7. 8. 7. 8. 7

O Thou, Who Hast of Thy Pure Grace

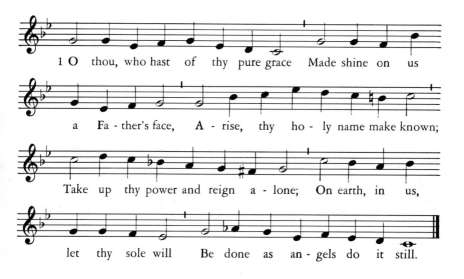

1 O thou, who hast of thy pure grace Made shine on us a Fa-ther's face, A-rise, thy ho-ly name make known; Take up thy power and reign a-lone; On earth, in us, let thy sole will Be done as an-gels do it still.

2 O King and Father, kind and dread,
Give us this day our daily bread;
Forgive us, who have learned to bless
Our enemies, all trespasses;
Spare us temptation, let us be
From Satan set forever free.

3 Thine is the kingdom, unto thee
Shall bow in homage every knee;
And thine the power; no power shall be
That is not overcome by thee;
The glory thine, by every tongue
Thy praise shall be forever sung. Amen.

A-men.

Text: Martin H. Franzmann (1907 –)
Tune: **Vater unser** *(Geistliche Lieder,* Leipzig, 1539)

8. 8. 8. 8. 8. 8

Have no anxiety about anything, but in everything by prayer and supplication with thanksgiving let your requests be made known to God.
Philippians 4:6

In Thee Is Gladness

1 In thee is glad - ness A - mid all sad - ness, Je - sus,
Sun - shine of my heart. By thee are giv - en the gifts of
heav - en, Thou the true Re - deem - er art. Our souls thou
wak - est, Our bonds thou break - est, Who trusts thee
sure - ly Has built se - cure - ly, He stands for - ev - er: Al - le - lu -
ia! Our hearts are pin - ing To see thy shin - ing, Dy - ing or
liv - ing To thee are cleav - ing, Naught can us sev - er: Al - le - lu - ia!

2 If he is ours,
We fear no powers,
Not of earth nor sin nor death.
He sees and blesses
In worst distresses,
He can change them with a breath.
Wherefore the story
Tell of his glory
With heart and voices,

All heaven rejoices
In him forever:
Alleluia!
We shout for gladness,
Triumph o'er sadness,
Love him and praise him
And still shall raise him
Glad hymns forever:
Alleluia!

Text: Johann Lindemann (1549−c. 1631); trans. Catherine Winkworth (1829−78)
Tune: **In dir ist Freude**, Giovanni Giacomo Gastoldi, 1591   5. 5. 7. D. 5. 5. 5. 5. 5. 4. D

Immortal, Invisible, God Only Wise

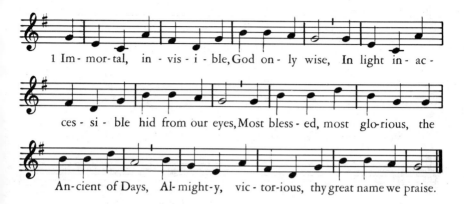

1 Im-mor-tal, in-vis-i-ble, God on-ly wise, In light in-ac-ces-si-ble hid from our eyes, Most bless-ed, most glo-rious, the An-cient of Days, Al-might-y, vic-tor-ious, thy great name we praise.

2 Unresting, unhasting, and silent as light,
   Nor wanting, nor wasting, thou rulest in might;
   Thy justice like mountains high soaring above
   Thy clouds which are fountains of goodness and love.

3 To all life thou givest — to both great and small —
   In all life thou livest, the true Life of all;
   We blossom and flourish as leaves on the tree
   And wither and perish — but naught changes thee.

4 Great Father of glory, pure Father of light,
   Thine angels adore thee, all veiling their sight;
   All laud we would render: O help us to see
   'Tis only the splendor of light that hides thee.

Text: Walter Chalmers Smith (1824 – 1908), cento, alt.
Tune: **St. Denio** (Traditional Welsh tune)

11. 11. 11. 11

O sing to the Lord a new song, for he has done marvelous things! His right hand and his holy arm have gotten him victory. The Lord has made known his victory, he has revealed his vindication in the sight of the nations. Psalm 98:1-2

Now

1 Now the si - lence Now the peace
2 Now the kneel - ing Now the plea

Now the emp - ty hands up - lift - ed
Now the Fa - ther's arms in wel - come

3 Now the hear - ing Now the power
4 Now the bod - y Now the blood

Now the ves - sel brimmed for pour - ing
Now the joy - ful cel - e - bra - tion

5 Now the wed - ding Now the songs

Now the heart for - giv - en leap - ing

6 Now the Spir - it's vis - i - ta - tion

Now the Son's e - piph - a - ny

Now the Fa - ther's bless - ing Now

Text: Jaroslav J. Vajda (1919–)
Tune: **Now**, Carl Schalk (1929–)

Jehovah, You We Glorify

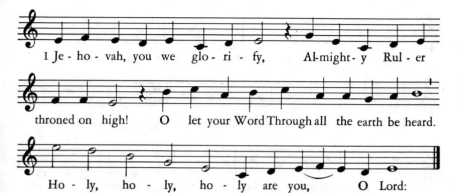

1 Jehovah, you we glorify, Almighty Ruler throned on high! O let your Word Through all the earth be heard. Holy, holy, holy are you, O Lord:

2 With gentle care you tend your flock;
Your Church, firm-founded on the Rock,
No powers dismay
Until your dreadful day.
Holy, holy, holy are you, O Lord!

3 Christ's lordship to all men reveal.
All nations, at his naming, kneel.
All saints, upraise
Your song of loving praise:
Holy, holy, holy are you, O Lord!

4 Around your throne the countless throng
At last in triumph swell the song
While cherubim
Reply to seraphim:
Holy, holy, holy are you, O Lord!

Text: Johan Olof Wallin (1779–1839); trans. composite 1925 and 1968
Tune: **Ter sanctus** (*Rostockerhandboken*, 1529)   8. 8. 4. 6. 10

Let the word of Christ dwell in you richly, as you teach and admonish one another in all wisdom, and as you sing psalms and hymns and spiritual songs with thankfulness in your hearts to God. Colossians 3:16

Only-Begotten, Word of God Eternal

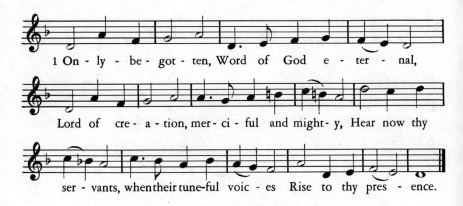

1 On - ly - be - got - ten, Word of God e - ter - nal,
Lord of cre - a - tion, mer - ci - ful and might - y, Hear now thy
ser - vants, when their tune-ful voic - es Rise to thy pres - ence.

2 Holy this temple where our Lord is dwelling,
This is none other than the gate of heaven;
Strangers and pilgrims, seeking homes eternal,
Pass through its portals.

3 Lord, we beseech thee, as we throng thy temple,
By thy past blessings, by thy present bounty,
Smile on thy children, and with tender mercy
Hear our petitions.

4 God in Three Persons, Father everliving,
Son coeternal, ever-blessèd Spirit,
Thine be the glory, praise, and adoration,
Now and forever. Amen.

A-men.

Text: Anonymous 9th-century Office hymn; trans. Maxwell J. Blacker (1822 – 88), cento, alt.
Tune: **Iste confessor** (Rouen Church tune)   11. 11. 11. 5

Beloved, do not be surprised at the fiery ordeal
which comes upon you to prove you, as though
something strange were happening to you. But
rejoice insofar as you share Christ's sufferings,
that you may also rejoice and be glad when his
glory is revealed. 1 Peter 4:12-13

Thank the Lord, for He Is Good

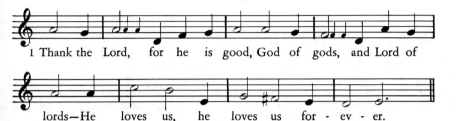

1 Thank the Lord, for he is good, God of gods, and Lord of lords—He loves us, he loves us for-ev-er.

2 See the wonders of his hands,
   Stars and heavens, earth and seas—

3 Israel was once enslaved,
   But he opened the Red Sea path—

4 Led his people the desert through,
   Mighty foes, he crushed them all—

5 Once no people, now his own,
   Homes once lost and left, restored—

6 Look, you people, people of God,
   Servants free, give him your hand—

7 Food to eat and air to breathe,
   Work to do, give thanks to him—

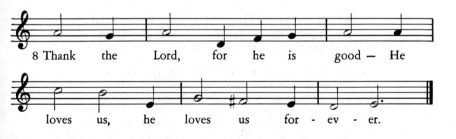

8 Thank the Lord, for he is good — He loves us, he loves us for-ev-er.

Text: Jaroslav J. Vajda (1919–)
Tune: **He Loves Us Forever**, Paul G. Bunjes (1914–)   7. 7 with refrain

O Fearful Place, Where He Who Knows Our Heart

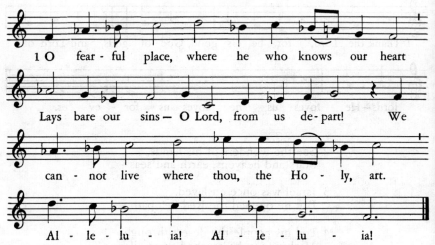

1 O fear-ful place, where he who knows our heart

Lays bare our sins— O Lord, from us de-part! We

can-not live where thou, the Ho-ly, art.

Al - le - lu - ia! Al - le - lu - ia!

2 O house of God, where angel troops descend
From heaven to man and on his saints attend;
Here let us sing the song that knows no end:

3 O gate of heaven, where God's almighty Word,
Big with forgiveness, constantly is heard,
And God's elect to shouts of praise are stirred:

4 O Son of God, who diedst our life to win,
Here in this house we died thy death to sin,
And from the dead with thee have raisèd been.

5 Thy servants here took our young life in hand
And taught us all that thy love did command
And made us in thy Spirit's strength to stand.

6 Thy body given and thy blood outpoured
In bread and wine here we have tasted, Lord;
For this thy gift forever be adored!

7 O God Almighty, gracious Three in One,
In this thy house let praise to thee be done
Until we join in heaven's high unison:
Alleluia! Alleluia! Amen.

A-men.

Text: Martin H. Franzmann (1907 –)
Tune: **Mission**, Richard Hillert (1923 –)

10. 10. 10 with alleluias

The following hymn may also be used:
772 Only-Begotten, Word of God Eternal

Go Labor On

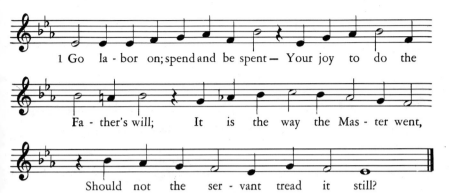

1 Go la - bor on; spend and be spent — Your joy to do the
Fa - ther's will; It is the way the Mas - ter went,
Should not the ser - vant tread it still?

2 Go labor on; 'tis not for naught;
Your earthly loss is heavenly gain;
Men heed you, love you, praise you not?
The Master praises — what are men?

3 Go labor on, while it is day,
The world's dark night is hastening on;
Speed, speed your work, cast sloth away;
It is not thus that souls are won.

4 Men die in darkness at your side,
Without a hope to cheer the tomb;
Take up the torch and wave it wide,
The torch that lights time's thickest gloom.

5 Toil on, faint not, keep watch, and pray;
Be wise the erring soul to win;
Go forth into the world's highway,
Compel the wanderer to come in.

6 Toil on, and in your toil rejoice;
For toil comes rest, for exile home;
Soon shall you hear the Bridegroom's voice,
The midnight cry, "Behold, I come!"

Text: Horatius Bonar (1808 – 89), cento, alt.
Tune: **Song 34**, Orlando Gibbons (1583 – 1625)   LM

The Voice of God Is Calling

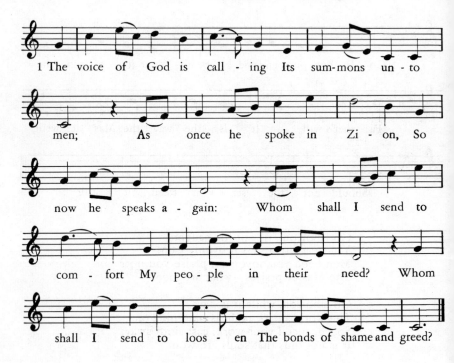

1 The voice of God is call - ing Its sum-mons un - to

men; As once he spoke in Zi - on, So

now he speaks a - gain: Whom shall I send to

com - fort My peo - ple in their need? Whom

shall I send to loos - en The bonds of shame and greed?

2 I hear my people crying
In cot and mine and slum;
No field or mart is silent,
No city street is dumb.
I see my people falling
In darkness and despair.
Whom shall I send to shatter
The fetters which they bear?

3 We heed, O Lord, thy summons
And answer: Here are we!
Send us upon thine errand!
Let us thy servants be!
Our strength is dust and ashes,
Our years a passing hour;
But thou canst use our weakness
To magnify thy power.

4 From ease and plenty save us,
From pride of place absolve;
Purge us of low desire,
Lift us to high resolve.
Teach us and make us holy,
Teach us thy will and way;
Speak, and behold we answer!
Command, and we obey!

5 Great God of earth and heaven,
To thee our songs we raise;
To thee be glory given
And everlasting praise:
We joyfully confess thee,
Eternal Triune God;
We magnify, we bless thee,
And spread thy praise abroad. Amen.

A-men.

Text: John Haynes Holmes (1879 – 1964) †
Tune: **Cormac** (Traditional Irish tune)

7. 6. 7. 6. D

The Church *SOCIAL CONCERN*

777

O Fount of Good, to Own Thy Love

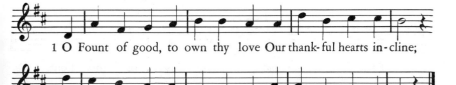

1 O Fount of good, to own thy love Our thank-ful hearts in-cline;

What can we ren-der, Lord, to thee, When all the worlds are thine?

2 But thou hast needy brethren here,
Partakers of thy grace,
Whose names thou wilt thyself
confess
Before the Father's face.

3 In each sad accent of distress
Thy pleading voice is heard;
In them thou mayest be clothed
and fed,
And visited and cheered.

4 Help us then, Lord, thy yoke
to wear,
And joy to do thy will;
Each other's burdens gladly bear,
The law of love fulfill.

5 Thy face with reverence and
with love
We in thy poor would see;
And while we minister to them,
Would do it as to thee.

Text: Philip Doddridge (1702 – 51) and Edmund Osler (1798 – 1863) †
Tune: **Song 67**, Orlando Gibbons (1583 – 1625)

CM

778

God of Grace and God of Glory

1 God of grace and God of glo-ry, On thy peo-ple
pour thy power; Crown thine an-cient church 's sto-ry;
Bring her bud to glo-rious flower. Grant us wis-dom,
Grant us cour-age, For the fac-ing of this hour,
For the fac - - ing of this hour.

2 Lo! the hosts of evil round us
Scorn thy Christ, assail his ways!
From the fears that long have bound us
Free our hearts to faith and praise.
Grant us wisdom,
Grant us courage,
For the living of these days.

3 Cure thy children's warring madness;
Bend our pride to thy control;
Shame our wanton, selfish gladness,
Rich in things and poor in soul.
Grant us wisdom,
Grant us courage,
Lest we miss thy kingdom's goal.

4 Set our feet on lofty places;
　Gird our lives that they may be
　Armored with all Christ-like graces
　In the fight to set men free.
　Grant us wisdom,
　Grant us courage,
　That we fail not man nor thee.

5 Save us from weak resignation
　To the evils we deplore;
　Let the gift of thy salvation
　Be our glory evermore.
　Grant us wisdom,
　Grant us courage,
　Serving thee whom we adore.

Text: Harry Emerson Fosdick (1878–) †
Tune: **Cwm Rhonda,** John Hughes (1873–1932)

8. 7. 8. 7. 4. 4. 7. 7

The Church *SOCIAL CONCERN*

779

Lord of All Nations, Grant Me Grace

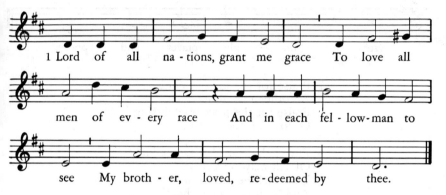

1 Lord of all na-tions, grant me grace To love all men of ev-ery race And in each fel-low-man to see My broth-er, loved, re-deemed by thee.

2 Break down the wall that would divide
　Thy children, Lord, on every side.
　Let me seek first my neighbor's good
　In bonds of Christian brotherhood.

3 Forgive me, Lord, where I have erred
　By loveless act and thoughtless word.
　Make me to see the wrong I do
　Will crucify my Lord anew.

4 Give me thy courage, Lord, to speak
　Whenever strong oppress the weak.
　Should I myself the victim be,
　Help me forgive, remembering thee.

5 With thine own love may I be filled
　And by thy Holy Spirit willed,
　That all I touch, where'er I be,
　May be divinely touched by thee.

Text: Olive Wise Spannaus (1916–)
Tune: **Beatus vir** (Slovak tune, 1561)

LM

We Lift Our Hearts, O Father

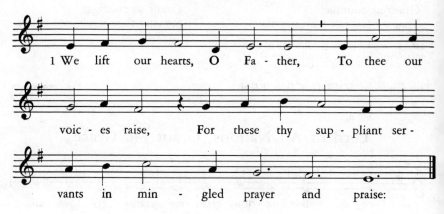

1 We lift our hearts, O Fa - ther, To thee our voic - es raise, For these thy sup - pliant ser - vants in min - gled prayer and praise:

2 Praise for the joy of loving,
All other joys above,
Praise for the priceless blessing
Of love's response to love;

3 Prayer that the glad surrender
Of self may perfect be,
That each be one with other,
And both be one in thee;

4 Prayer that thou wilt accomplish
The promise of today
And crown the years with blessing
That shall not pass away;

5 Praise for the hope most glorious
That looks beyond the veil,
Where faith and hope shall vanish,
But love shall never fail.

Text: Edward Ashurst Welch (1860—1932)
Tune: **We Lift Our Hearts**, Carl Schalk (1929—)

7. 6. 7. 6

Do you not know that your body is a temple of
the Holy Spirit within you, which you have from
God? You are not your own; you were bought
with a price. So glorify God in your body.
1 Corinthians 6:19-20

O Lord of Love, Whose Truth Our Lives Adorn

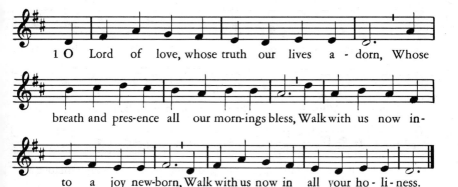

1 O Lord of love, whose truth our lives a - dorn, Whose
breath and pres-ence all our morn-ings bless, Walk with us now into a joy new-born, Walk with us now in all your ho - li - ness.

2 Lead us to love in truth, as you have done.
Fill our renewing lives with joy unfurled.
Revive our persons with your victor's song
And send us singing into your own world.

3 Now round your throne of grace be said our prayer!
Now round your streaming light be sung our praise!
O Savior, O Divine One lifted there,
Give us your rising love — our spirits raise!

Text: Walter C. Riess (1925 –), cento
Tune: **Sursum corda**, Alfred Morton Smith (1879 –)   10. 10. 10. 10

O God, from whom all holy desires, all good
counsels, and all just works do proceed, give
unto Thy servants that peace which the world
cannot give, that our hearts may be set to obey
Thy commandments, and also that by Thee,
we, being defended from the fear of our enemies,
may pass our time in rest and quietness; through
the merits of Jesus Christ, our Savior, who liveth
and reigneth with Thee and the Holy Spirit, one
God, forever and ever. Amen.

Our Father, by Whose Name

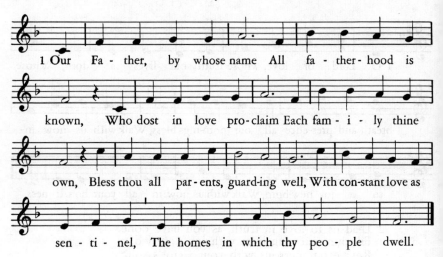

1 Our Fa - ther, by whose name All fa - ther - hood is
known, Who dost in love pro - claim Each fam - i - ly thine
own, Bless thou all par - ents, guard - ing well, With con - stant love as
sen - ti - nel, The homes in which thy peo - ple dwell.

2 O Christ, thyself a child
Within an earthly home,
With heart still undefiled,
Thou didst to manhood come;
Our children bless in every place,
That they may all behold thy face,
And knowing thee may grow in grace.

3 O Spirit, who dost bind
Our hearts in unity,
Who teachest us to find
The love from self set free,
In all our hearts such love increase,
That every home, by this release,
May be the dwelling place of peace.

Text: F. Bland Tucker (1895 –)
Tune: **Rhosymedre**, John Edwards (1806 – 85)   6. 6. 6. 6. 8. 8. 8

"If you love me, you will keep my commandments. And I will pray the Father, and he will give you another Counselor, to be with you forever, even the Spirit of truth, whom the world cannot receive, because it neither sees him nor knows him; you know him, for he dwells with you, and will be in you." John 14:15-17

God, My Lord, My Strength

1 God, my Lord, my Strength, my Place of
Hid-ing And con-fid-ing In all needs
by night and day; Let foes sur-round me, Let
Sa-tan mark his prey, God shall have his way.

2 Christ in me, and I am freed for living
And forgiving,
Heart of flesh for lifeless stone;
Now bold to serve him,
Now cheered his love to own,
Nevermore alone.

3 Up, weak knees and spirit bowed in sorrow!
No tomorrow
Shall arrive to beat you down;
God goes before you,
And angels all around,
On your head a crown!

Text: Author unknown, cento; paraphr. Jaroslav J. Vajda (1919 –)
Tune: **Pán Bůh** (The Prague Gradual, 1567)   10. 4. 7. 5. 6. 5

For thou dost not give me up to Sheol, or let thy godly one see the Pit. Thou dost show me the path of life; in thy presence there is fullness of joy, in thy right hand are pleasures forevermore. Psalm 16:10-11

O God of Earth and Altar

1 O God of earth and al - tar, Bow down and hear our
cry, Our earth- ly rul - ers fal - ter, Our peo- ple drift and
die; The walls of gold en - tomb us, The swords of scorn divide, Take not thy thun - der from us, But take a - way our pride.

2 From all that terror teaches,
From lies of tongue and pen,
From all the easy speeches
That comfort cruel men,
From sale and profanation
Of honor and the sword,
From sleep and from damnation,
Deliver us, good Lord!

3 Tie in a living tether
The prince and priest and thrall,*
Bind all our lives together,
Smite us and save us all;
In ire and exultation
Aflame with faith, and free,
Lift up a living nation,
A single sword to thee. Amen.

A-men.

* thrall = a person in bondage

Text: Gilbert Keith Chesterton (1874 – 1936)
Tune: **King's Lynn** (Traditional English tune)

7. 6. 7. 6. D

Grant Peace, We Pray, in Mercy, Lord

Grant peace, we pray, in mer - cy, Lord, Peace in our time O send us! For there is none on earth but thee, None oth - er to de - fend us. Thou on - ly, Lord, canst fight for us. A - - - men.

Text: Medieval antiphon recast by Martin Luther (1483 – 1546); trans. composite, 1952
Tune: **Verleih uns Frieden** (Medieval tune; Wittenberg, 1529)   8. 7. 8. 7. 8

Almighty God, give us grace that we may cast away the works of darkness and put upon ourselves the armor of light, now in the time of this mortal life, in which Thy Son Jesus Christ came to visit us in great humility, that in the Last Day, when He shall come again in His glorious majesty to judge both the quick and the dead, we may rise to the life immortal; through Jesus Christ, Thy Son, our Lord. Amen.

Lord of Our Life and God of Our Salvation

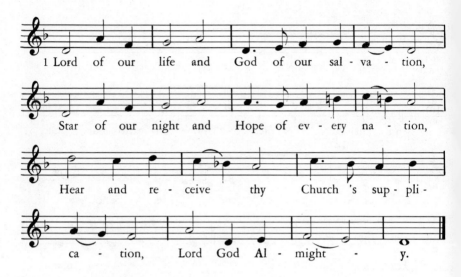

1 Lord of our life and God of our sal - va - tion,

Star of our night and Hope of ev - ery na - tion,

Hear and re - ceive thy Church 's sup - pli -

ca - tion, Lord God Al - might - y.

2 See round thine ark the hungry billows curling;
   See how thy foes their banners are unfurling;
   Lord, while their darts envenomed they are hurling,
   Thou canst preserve us.

3 Lord, thou canst help when earthly armor faileth,
   Lord, thou canst save when deadly sin assaileth;
   Christ, o'er thy Church nor death nor hell prevaileth;
   Grant us thy peace, Lord.

4 Peace in our hearts, our evil thoughts assuaging;
   Peace in thy Church, where brothers are engaging;
   Peace, when the world its busy war is waging:
   Calm thy foes' raging.

5 Grant us thy help till backward they are driven,
   Grant them thy truth that they may be forgiven;
   Grant peace on earth, and after we have striven,
   Peace in thy heaven. Amen.

A-men.

Text: Matthäus A. von Löwenstern (1594–1648); paraphr. Philip Pusey (1799–1855), alt.
Tune: **Iste confessor** (Rouen Church tune)   11. 11. 11. 5

O God of Love, O King of Peace

1 O God of love, O King of peace, Make
wars through-out the world to cease; The wrath of sin - ful
man re - strain; Give peace, O God, give peace a - gain.

2 Remember, Lord, your works of old,
The wonders that our fathers told,
Remember not our sins' dark stain;
Give peace, O God, give peace again.

3 Whom shall we trust but you, O Lord?
Where rest but on your faithful Word?
None ever called on you in vain.
Give peace, O God, give peace again.

4 Where saints and angels dwell above,
All hearts are knit in holy love;
O bind us in that heavenly chain.
Give peace, O God, give peace again. Amen.

A-men.

Text: Henry Williams Baker (1821—77)
Tune: **Pax** (Swedish *Koralbok,* 1697)

LM

Another hymn for peace may be found in The Lutheran Hymnal
582 God, Lord of Sabaoth, Thou Who Ordainest

Surely he has borne our griefs and carried our
sorrows; yet we esteemed him stricken, smitten
by God, and afflicted. But he was wounded for
our transgressions, he was bruised for our
iniquities; upon him was the chastisement that
made us whole, and with his stripes we are
healed. Isaiah 53:4-5

Father, We Praise Thee, Now the Night Is Over

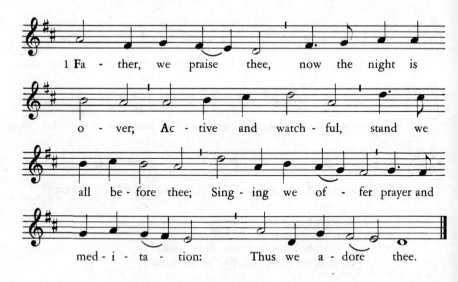

1 Fa - ther, we praise thee, now the night is o - ver; Ac - tive and watch - ful, stand we all be - fore thee; Sing - ing we of - fer prayer and med - i - ta - tion: Thus we a - dore thee.

2 Monarch of all things, fit us for thy mansions;
Banish our weakness, health and wholeness sending;
Bring us to heaven, where thy saints united
Joy without ending.

3 All-holy Father, Son, and equal Spirit,
Trinity blessèd, send us thy salvation;
Thine is the glory, gleaming and resounding
Through all creation. Amen.

A-men.

Text: Ascr. Gregory the Great (540–604); trans. Percy Dearmer (1867–1936)
Tune: **Christe sanctorum** (La Feillée, *Méthode du plain-chant*, 1782)   11. 11. 11. 5

Nevertheless I am continually with thee; thou dost hold my right hand. Thou dost guide me with thy counsel, and afterward thou wilt receive me to glory. Whom have I in heaven but thee? And there is nothing upon earth that I desire besides thee. My flesh and my heart may fail, but God is the strength of my heart and my portion forever. Psalm 73:23-26

When Morning Gilds the Skies

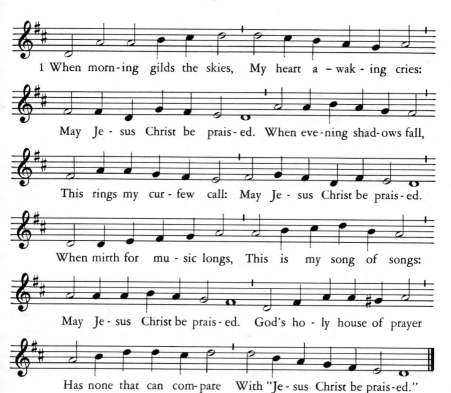

1 When morn-ing gilds the skies, My heart a – wak-ing cries:

May Je - sus Christ be prais-ed. When eve-ning shad-ows fall,

This rings my cur-few call: May Je - sus Christ be prais-ed.

When mirth for mu-sic longs, This is my song of songs:

May Je-sus Christ be prais-ed. God's ho - ly house of prayer

Has none that can com-pare With "Je - sus Christ be prais-ed."

2 To him, my highest and best,
Sing I, when love-possessed:
May Jesus Christ be praisèd.
Whate'er my hands begin,
This blessing shall break in:
May Jesus Christ be praisèd.
No lovelier antiphon
In all high heaven is known
Than "Jesus Christ be praisèd."
There to the eternal Word
The eternal psalm is heard:
"O Jesus Christ be praisèd."

3 You nations of mankind,
In this your concord find:
May Jesus Christ be praisèd.
Let all the earth around
Ring joyous with the sound:
May Jesus Christ be praisèd.
Sing, suns and stars of space,
Sing, ye who see his face,
Sing "Jesus Christ be praisèd."
God's whole creation o'er,
For aye and evermore,
Shall Jesus Christ be praisèd.

Text: Author unknown, 19th century; trans. Robert Bridges (1844 – 1930)
Tune: **O Seigneur** (*Genevan Psalter,* 1551)   6. 6. 7. 6. 6. 7. D

Before the Ending of the Day

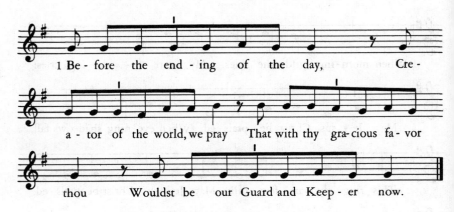

1 Be - fore the end - ing of the day, Cre -
a - tor of the world, we pray That with thy gra - cious fa - vor
thou Wouldst be our Guard and Keep - er now.

2 From all ill dreams defend our sight,
From fears and terrors of the night:
Drive far away our wily foe
That spot of sin we may not know.

3 O Father, this we ask be done
Through Jesus Christ, thine only Son,
Who, with the Holy Ghost and thee,
Both lives and reigns eternally. Amen.

A - men.

Text: Compline Office hymn, c. 8th century; trans. John Mason Neale (1818—66), alt.
Tune: Jam lucis (Benedictine plainsong, Mode VI)   LM

Have this mind among yourselves, which you
have in Christ Jesus, who, though he was in
the form of God, did not count equality with God
a thing to be grasped, but emptied himself,
taking the form of a servant, being born in the
likeness of men. And being found in human form
he humbled himself and became obedient unto
death, even death on a cross. Philippians 2:5-8

I place music next to theology and give it the
highest praise. Martin Luther (1541)

Greet, Man, the Swiftly Changin

792

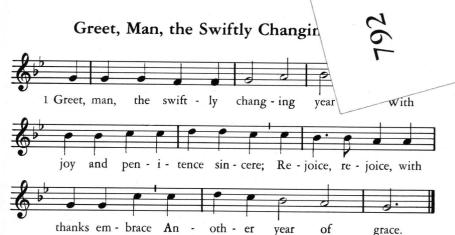

1 Greet, man, the swift-ly chang-ing year with
joy and pen-i-tence sin-cere; Re-joice, re-joice, with
thanks em-brace An-oth-er year of grace.

2 Remember now the Son of God
And how he shed his infant
blood;
Rejoice, rejoice, with thanks
embrace
Another year of grace.

3 This *Jesus,* come to wage sin's war,
This name of names for us he bore;
Rejoice, rejoice, with thanks
embrace
Another year of grace.

4 Well-proved his love for many a
year,
He brought us safe through dark
and clear;
Rejoice, rejoice, with thanks
embrace
Another year of grace.

5 His love abundant far exceeds
The volume of a whole year's
needs;
Rejoice, rejoice, with thanks
embrace
Another year of grace.

6 With such a Lord to lead our way
In hazard and prosperity,
What need we fear in earth or
space
In this new year of grace!

7 All glory be to God
on high
And peace on earth to all
men nigh;
Rejoice, rejoice, with thanks
embrace
Another year of grace.

8 God Father, Son, and Spirit dear,
To all our pleas incline thine ear;
Upon our lives rich blessing trace
In this new year of grace. Amen.

A-men.

Text: Author unknown, cento; trans. Jaroslav J. Vajda (1919—)
Tune: **Rok novy** (*Zavorka Kancional,* 1602)

8. 8. 8. 6

This hymn is suitable also for Circumcision and Holy Name.

Forgive Us, Lord, for Shallow Thankfulness

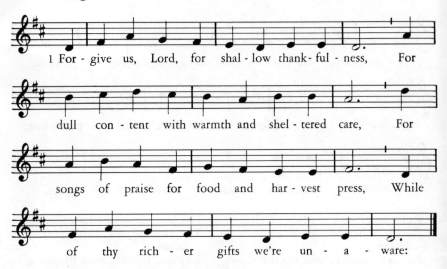

1 For - give us, Lord, for shal - low thank - ful - ness, For
dull con - tent with warmth and shel - tered care, For
songs of praise for food and har - vest press, While
of thy rich - er gifts we're un - a - ware:

2 Teach us to thank thee, Lord, for love and grace,
   For life and vision and a purpose clear,
   For Christ, thy Son, and for each human face
   That shows thy message ever new and near.

3 Forgive us, Lord, for selfish thanks and praise,
   For word that speaks at variance with deed;
   Forgive our thanks for walking pleasant ways
   Unmindful of a broken brother's need:

4 Teach us, O Lord, true thankfulness divine,
   That gives as Christ gave, never counting cost,
   That knows no barrier of "mine" and "thine,"
   Assured that only what's withheld is lost.

5 Forgive us, Lord, for feast that knows not fast,
   For joy in things the while we starve the soul,
   For walls and wars that hide thy mercies vast
   And mar our vision of the kingdom goal:

6 Open our eyes to glimpse thy love's intent,
   Our minds and hearts to plumb its depth and height;
   May thankfulness be days in service spent,
   Reflection of Christ's life and love and light. Amen.

A-men.

Text: William Watkins Reid Sr. (1890–)
Tune: **Sursum corda**, Alfred M. Smith (1879–)

10. 10. 10. 10

Sing to the Lord of Harvest

1 Sing to the Lord of har-vest, Sing songs of love and praise; With joy-ful hearts and voic-es Your al-le-lu-ias raise. By him the roll-ing sea-sons In fruit-ful or-der move; Sing to the Lord of har-vest A joy-ous song of love.

2 By him the clouds drop fatness,
The deserts bloom and spring,
The hills leap up in gladness,
The valleys laugh and sing.
He filleth with his fullness
All things with large increase,
He crowns the year with goodness,
With plenty and with peace.

3 Bring to his sacred altar
The gifts his goodness gave,
The golden sheaves of harvest,
The souls he died to save.
Your hearts lay down before him
When at his feet you fall,
And with your lives adore him,
Who gave his life for all.

Text: John Samuel Bewley Monsell (1811—75)
Tune: **Wie lieblich ist der Maien,** Johann Steurlein (1546—1613)   7. 6. 7. 6. D

Thou art holy, enthroned on the praises of Israel. In thee our fathers trusted; they trusted, and thou didst deliver them. To thee they cried, and were saved; in thee they trusted, and were not disappointed. Psalm 22:3-5

Sing praises to God, sing praises! Sing praises to our King, sing praises! Psalm 47:6

Indexes

Index of Hymns of the Week

Advent I
Savior of the nations, come — 701

Advent II
Lo! He comes with clouds
    descending — 702

Christmas Day
We praise, O Christ, your holy name — 708

Second Sunday After Christmas
From east to west, from shore
    to shore — 709

Epiphany I
Of the Father's love begotten — 721

Epiphany II
The only Son from heaven — 722

Transfiguration
O wondrous type! O vision fair — 723

Lent III (Oculi)
Lord of our life and God
    of our salvation — 786

Lent V (Judica)
The royal banners forward go — 729, 730

Lent VI (Palmarum)
Ride on, ride on in majesty! — 727

Easter III (Jubilate)
With high delight — 734

Ascension
See God to heaven ascending — 744

Easter VI (Exaudi)
O Love, how deep, how broad,
    how high — 750

Trinity I
Now let us pray to God
    the Holy Ghost — 753

Trinity XII
O thou, who once in Galilee — 751

Trinity XX
O kingly love, that faithfully — 757

Index of Translated Hymns

French
Les anges dans nos campagnes / Angels we have heard on high 711

Gaelic (Irish)
Atomriug Indiu / I bind unto myself today (paraphr.) 746

German
Beim frühen Morgenlicht / When morning gilds the skies 789
Christ ist erstanden / Christ is arisen 741
Christe, du Beistand deiner Kreuzgemeine / Lord of our life
   and God of our salvation (paraphr.) 786
Der du, Herr Jesu, Ruh und Rast / Lord Jesus, who, our souls to save 732
Gelobet seist du, Jesu Christ / We praise, O Christ, your holy name 708
Gott fähret auf gen Himmel / See God to heaven ascending 744
Herr Christ, der einig Gotts Sohn / The only Son from heaven 722
Herr Gott, dich loben wir / Lord God, thy praise we sing 745
In dir ist Freude / In thee is gladness 768
In dulci jubilo (macaronic) / In dulci jubilo (macaronic) 714
Lobt Gott, ihr Christen allzugleich / Let all together praise our God 712
Mit Freuden zart / With high delight 734
Nun bitten wir den heiligen Geist / Now let us pray to God
   the Holy Ghost 753
O Heiland, reiss die Himmel auf / O Savior, rend the heavens wide 706
Verleih uns Frieden gnädiglich / Grant peace, we pray, in mercy, Lord 785

Greek
Αἴσωμεν πάντες λαοί / Come, ye faithful, raise the strain 738
'Αναστάσεως ἡμέρα / The day of resurrection 739
Σιγησάτω πᾶσα σὰρξ βροτεία / Let all mortal flesh keep silence
   (paraphr.) 766

Italian
Descendi, amor santo / Come down, O Love divine 755

Latin
A solis ortus cardine / From east to west, from shore to shore 709
Ad regias agni dapes / At the Lamb's high feast we sing 733
Adeste fideles / O come, all ye faithful 710
Caelestis formam gloriae / O wondrous type! O vision fair 723

Christe cunctorum dominator alme / Only-begotten, Word of God eternal 772
Claro paschali gaudio (cento from Aurora lucis rutilat) / That Easter day
 with joy was bright 737
Conditor alme siderum / Creator of the stars of night 703
Corde natus ex parentis / Of the Father's love begotten 721
Da pacem, Domine (via German Verleih uns Frieden gnädiglich) / Grant
 peace, we pray, in mercy, Lord 785
En clara vox redarguit / Hark! A thrilling voice is sounding 704
Finita iam sunt proelia / The strife is o'er, the battle done 740
In dulci jubilo (macaronic) / In dulci jubilo (macaronic) 714
Nocte surgentes vigilemus omnes / Father, we praise thee,
 now the night is over 788
Nunc angelorum / The glorious angels came today 718
O amor quam exstaticus / O love, how deep, how broad, how high 750
O filii et filiae / O sons and daughters of the King 735
Pange, lingua, gloriosi Proelium / Sing, my tongue, the glorious battle 728
Quem pastores laudavere / He whom shepherd men came praising 718
Qui jacuisti mortuus (via German Der du, Herr Jesu, Ruh und Rast) /
 Lord Jesus, who, our souls to save 732
Resonet in laudibus / God's own Son is born a child 718
Te Deum laudamus (via German Herr Gott, dich loben wir) / Lord God,
 thy praise we sing 745
Te lucis ante terminum / Before the ending of the day 790
Veni, Redemptor gentium / Savior of the nations, come 701
Vexilla regis prodeunt / The royal banners forward go 729, 730
Victimae paschali / Christians, to the Paschal Victim 741

Slovak

Pán Bůh jest má síla i doufáni / God, my Lord, my Strength,
 my Place of hiding 783
Rok nový zase k nám přišel / Greet, man, the swiftly changing year 791

Swedish

Vi lova dig, o store Gud / Jehovah, you we glorify 771

Index of Composers and Sources

American tune, early
Lord, Revive Us 752

Augsburg, 1666
O Heiland, reiss die
Himmel auf 706

Beck, Theodore A. (1929–)
Speak forth thy Word 760

Bender, Jan O. (1909–)
Wittenberg New 758

Bohemian Brethren
14th-century tune; 1531
Erstanden ist der heilig
Christ 740
15th-century tune
Sonne der Gerechtigkeit 733
Kirchengeseng, 1566
Mit Freuden zart 734

Bunjes, Paul G. (1914–)
He Loves Us Forever 773

Crüger, Johann (1598–1662)
Zeuch ein zu deinen Toren 744

Dutch traditional tune
In Babilone 754
Vruechten (17th century) 742

Eccard, Johann (1553–1611)
The King's Banner (ascr.) 729

Edwards, John (1806–85)
Rhosymedre 782

Enchiridion, Erfurt, 1524
Christum wir sollen
loben schon 709
Gelobet seist du,
Jesu Christ 708

English traditional tunes
15th century: Deo gracias 723, 750
16th century (ballad):
Greensleeves 719
Forest Green 715
King's Lynn 756, 784

Farrant, Richard (d. 1581)
Farrant (ascr.) 763

French traditional tunes
Gloria 711

Picardy 702, 766
O filii et filiae (Mode II) 735

Gastoldi, Giovanni Giacomo
(c. 1550–1622)
In dir ist Freude 768

Geistliche Lieder, Leipzig, 1539
Vater unser 767

Genevan Psalter, 1551
Donne secours (Psalm 12) 749
O Seigneur (Psalm 3) 789
Psalm 146 731

George, Graham (1912–)
The King's Majesty 727

German traditional tunes
Medieval; Wittenberg, 1529
Verleih uns Frieden 785
12th century: Christ ist
erstanden 741
13th century: Nun bitten wir 753
15th century: Dies est
laetitiae (variant) 720
15th century: Erfurt, 1524
Herr Christ, der einig
Gotts Sohn 722

Geystliche gesangk Buchleyn,
Wittenberg, 1524
Nun komm, der Heiden
Heiland 701

Gibbons, Orlando (1583–1625)
Song 20 762
Song 34 775
Song 67 777

Helder, Bartholomäus
(c. 1585–1635)
Ich freu mich in dem Herren 724

Herman, Nikolaus
(c. 1480–1561)
Erschienen ist der
herrlich Tag 737
Lobt Gott, ihr Christen
allzugleich 712

Hillert, Richard W. (1923–)
Kingly Love 757
Mission 761, 774

Salem 751
Shepherding 713

Horn, Johann (=Jan Roh)
  (c. 1490–1547)
  Gaudeamus pariter 738

Hughes, John (1873–1932)
  Cwm Rhondda 778

Ireland, John (1879–1962)
  Love Unknown 725

Irish traditional tunes
  Cormac 776
  St. Patrick's Breastplate 746

Kentucky Harmony, 1816
  Consolation 707

Klug's *Geistliche Lieder,*
  Wittenberg, 1535
  In dulci jubilo 714

La Feillée, *Méthode du plain-
  chant,* 1782
  Christe sanctorum 788

Lawes, Henry (1596–1662)
  Farley Castle (ascr.) 765

Luther, Martin (1483–1546)
  Te Deum 745

*Newe Deudsche Geistliche
  Gesenge,* Wittenberg, 1544
  Nun lasst uns den Leib
    begraben 732

Owen, William (1814–93)
  Bryn Calfaria 764

Piae Cantiones, 1582
  Tempus adest floridum
    (14th-century carol) 716

Plainsong
  Benedictine, Mode VI: Jam lucis 790
  Mode I, ascr. Wipo (d. c. 1050):
    Victimae paschali 741
  Mode V, 13th century:
    Divinum mysterium 721
  Sarum Mode I: Vexilla regis 730
  Sarum Mode IV: Conditor
    alme siderum 703

Prague Gradual, 1567
  Pán Bůh 783

Roh, Jan, cf. Horn, Johann

Rostockerhandboken, 1529
  Ter Sanctus 771

Rouen church tune
  Iste confessor 772, 786

Sateren, Leland B. (1913–)
  Marlee 726

Schalk, Carl F. (1929–)
  Fortunatus New 728
  Now 770
  We Lift Our Hearts 780

*Schlesisch Singebüchlein
  aus göttlicher Schrifft,* 1555
  Quem pastores 718

Slovak traditional tune
  Beatus vir (1561) 779

Smith, Alfred Morton (1879–)
  Sursum corda 781, 792

Southern Harmony, 1835
  Jefferson 705
  Pilgrim 748
  The Saints' Delight 759

Steurlein, Johann (1546–1613)
  Wie lieblich ist der Maien 793

Swedish *Koralbok,* 1697
  Pax (Ack, bliv hos oss) 787

Unknown source
  Adeste fideles 710
  Nunc angelorum 718

Vaughan Williams, Ralph
  (1872–1958)
  Down Ampney 755
  King's Weston 743

Vulpius, Melchior (c. 1570–1615)
  Das neugeborne Kindelein 717
  Gelobt sei Gott 736

Walther, Johann (1496–1570)
  Herzlich tut mich erfreuen
    (recast of 16th-cent. tune) 739

Weisse, Michael (c. 1480–1534)
  Freuen wir uns alle 704

Welsh traditional tune
  St. Denio 769

Williams, Thomas John
  (1869–1944)
  Ebenezer 747

Zavorka Kancional, 1602
  Rok nový 791

Metrical Index of Tunes

SM — 6.6.8.6

Song 20   762

CM — 8.6.8.6

Consolation   707
Farrant   763
Saints' Delight, The   759
Salem   751
Song 67   777

CMD

Pilgrim   748

LM — 8.8.8.8

Ack, bliv hos oss (Pax)   787
Agincourt Hymn (Deo gracias)   723, 750
Angel's Song (Song 34)   775
Beatus vir   779
Christum wir sollen loben schon   709
Conditor alme siderum
   (plainsong)   703
Deo gracias (Agincourt Hymn)   723, 750
Jam lucis (plainsong)   790
King's Banner, The   729
King's Majesty, The   727
Nun lasst uns den Leib begraben   732
O Heiland, reiss die Himmel auf   706
Pax (Ack, bliv hos oss)   787
Song 34 (Angel's Song)   775
Vexilla regis (plainsong)   730

LM with alleluia

Erschienen ist der herrlich Tag   737

LM with refrain

Kingly Love   757

LMD

Saint Patrick's Breastplate   746
Wittenberg New   758

5.5.7.D.5.5.5.5.5.4.D

In dir ist Freude   768

6.5.6.5.D

King's Weston   743

6.6.6.6.4.4.4.4

Love Unknown   725

6.6.6.6.6.6.5.5

In dulci jubilo   714

6.6.6.6.8.8

Marlee   726

6.6.6.6.8.8.8

Rhosymedre   782

6.6.7.6.6.7.D

O Seigneur   789

6.6.11.D

Down Ampney   755

6.7.6.7 with refrain

Vruechten   742

7.6.7.6

We Lift Our Hearts   780

7.6.7.6.D

Ave, virgo virginum
   (Gaudeamus pariter)
   (Trochaic)   738
Cormac   776
Gaudeamus pariter
   (Ave, virgo virginum)
   (Trochaic)   738
Herzlich tut mich erfreuen   739
Ich freu mich in dem Herren   724
King's Lynn   756, 784
Speak Forth Thy Word   760
Tempus adest floridum   716
Wie lieblich ist der Maien   793

7.6.7.6.6.6.7.7.6

Zeuch ein zu deinen Toren   744

7.6.7.6.7.7.5.7.7.6

Dies est laetitiae (variant form)   720

7.6.7.6.7.7.6

Herr Christ, der einig Gotts Sohn   722

7.7 with refrain

He Loves Us Forever   773

7.7.7.7

Nun komm, der Heiden Heiland   701

7.7.7.7 with refrain

Gloria (Iris; Westminster Carol)   711
Iris (Gloria; Westminster Carol)   711
Westminster Carol (Gloria; Iris)   711

7.7.7.7.4

Sonne der Gerechtigkeit   733

8.6.8.6.6

Lobt Gott, ihr Christen allzugleich   712
Shepherding   713

8.6.8.6.7.6.8.6
Forest Green 715

8.7.8.7
Freuen wir uns alle 704

8.7.8.7.4.4.4.7.7
Bryn Calfaria 764

8.7.8.7.4.4.7.7
Cwm Rhondda 778

8.7.8.7.6.8.6.7
Greensleeves 719

8.7.8.7.7.7
Psalm 146 731

8.7.8.7.8
Da pacem
(Verleih uns Frieden)
(plainsong) 785
Verleih uns Frieden
(Da pacem) (plainsong) 785

8.7.8.7.8.7
Fortunatus New 728
Picardy 702, 766

8.7.8.7.8.7.7
Divinum mysterium (plainsong) 721

8.7.8.7.D
Ebenezer (Ton-y-Botel) 747
In Babilone 754
Jefferson 705
Lord, Revive Us 752
Ton-y-Botel (Ebenezer) 747

8.7.8.8.4
Gelobet seist du, Jesu Christ 708

8.8.4.6.10
Ter Sanctus 771

8.8.8 with alleluias
Erstanden ist der heilig Christ 740
Gelobt sei Gott (Vulpius) 736
O filii et filiae 735
Vulpius (Gelobt sei Gott) 736

8.8.8.6
Rok nový 791

8.8.8.7
Quem pastores (Trochaic) 718

8.8.8.8.8.8
Das neugeborne Kindelein 717
Old 112th (Vater unser) 767
Vater unser (Old 112th) 767

8.8.8.8.8.8.8
Mit Freuden zart 734

10.4.7.5.6.5
Pán Bůh 783

10.9.11.9.4
Nun bitten wir 753

10.10.10 with alleluias
Mission 761, 774

10.10.10.10
Farley Castle 765
Sursum corda 781, 792

11.10.11.10
Donne secours 749

11.11
Resonet in laudibus 718

11.11.11.5
Christe sanctorum (plainsong) 788
Iste confessor (plainsong) 772, 786

11.11.11.11
Joanna (St. Denio) 769
St. Denio (Joanna) 769

Irregular
Adeste fideles (Portuguese Hymn) 710
Christ ist erstanden 741
Herr Gott, dich loben wir
(Te Deum) 745
Now 770
Nunc angelorum 718
Portuguese Hymn (Adeste fideles) 710
Te Deum (Herr Gott,
dich loben wir) 745
Victimae paschali (plainsong) 741

A Table of Metrical Psalms

Psalm	The Lutheran Hymnal	Psalm	The Lutheran Hymnal
1	414	98	87
12	260	100	13, 14, 44
23	368, 426, 431, 436	103	34, 39
24	73	104	17
31	435, 524	108	27
32	392	117	15
34	29	118	10
38	402	119	286
42	525	122	292
46	262	124	267
48	636	130	329
51	325, 398	136	570, *Worship Supplement,* No. 773
67	20, 500		
72	59, 511		
78	629	137	462
84	480	146	26
90	123	150	41, part of 39

A Table of Psalms for Chanting

Psalm	The Lutheran Hymnal	Psalm	The Lutheran Hymnal
23	662	100	666
92	663	121	665
95	page 33	130	664
98	667		

Index of Authors and Translators

Alexander, Cecil Frances, 1823 – 95
  I bind unto myself today (trans.)   746

Alington, Cyril Argentine, 1872 – 1955
  Good Christian men, rejoice and sing   736

Ambrose, St., 340 – 397
  Savior of the nations, come (ascr.)   701

Anonymous
  5th century
    That Easter day with joy was bright (Latin)   737
  6th century
    Hark! A thrilling voice is sounding (Latin)   704
  8th century
    Before the ending of the day (Latin)   790
  9th century
    Creator of the stars of night (Latin)   703
    Only-begotten, Word of God eternal (Latin)   772
  14th century
    God's own Son is born a child   718
    He whom shepherd men came praising (Latin)   718
    In dulci jubilo (Latin-German macaronic)   714
    The glorious angels came today (Latin)   718
  15th century
    O wondrous type, O vision fair (Latin)   723
  16th century
    O sons and daughters of the King (Latin)   735
  17th century
    At the Lamb's high feast we sing (Latin)   733
    God, my Lord, my Strength (Slovak)   783
    Greet, man, the swiftly changing year (Slovak)   791
    O Savior, rend the heavens wide (German)   706
    The strife is o'er, the battle done (Latin)   740
  18th century
    Angels we have heard on high (French)   711
    O come, all ye faithful (Latin)   710
  19th century
    When morning gilds the skies (German)   789

Baker, Henry Williams, 1821—77
    O God of love, O King of peace   787
    Of the Father's love begotten (adaptation of the J. M. Neale trans.) 721

Bianco da Siena, d. 1434
    Come down, O Love divine   755

Bickersteth, Edward Henry, 1825—1906
    Stand, soldier of the cross   762

Blacker, Maxwell Julius, 1822—88
    Only-begotten, Word of God eternal (trans.)   772

Bonar, Horatius, 1808—89
    Go labor on; spend, and be spent   775
    Here, O my Lord, I see thee face to face   765

Bouman, Herbert J. A., 1908—
    The glorious angels came today (trans.)   718

Bourne, George Hugh, 1840—1925
    Lord, enthroned in heavenly splendor   764

Bridges, Robert Seymour, 1844—1930
    When morning gilds the skies (trans.)   789

Brooks, Phillips, 1835—93
    O little town of Bethlehem   715

Brownlie, John, 1859—1925
    The King shall come when morning dawns   707

Buszin, Walter Edwin, 1899—
    Lord God, thy praise we sing (trans.)   745

Campbell, Robert, 1814—68
    At the Lamb's high feast we sing (trans.)   733

Caswall, Edward, 1818—78
    Hark! A thrilling voice is sounding (trans.)   704

Chesterton, Gilbert Keith, 1874—1936
    O God of earth and altar   784

Composite translations
    Christians, to the Paschal Victim   741
    Jehovah, you we glorify   771
    Now let us pray to God the Holy Ghost   753

Cook, Joseph Simpson, 1858—1933
    Gentle Mary laid her Child   716

Crossman, Samuel, c. 1624—83
    My song is love unknown   725

Cruciger, Elizabeth, c. 1500—35
    The only Son from heaven   722

Danker, William J., 1914 –
    The sending, Lord, springs from thy yearning heart   761

Dearmer, Percy, 1867 – 1936
    Father, we praise thee, now the night is over (trans.)   788

Dix, William Chatterton, 1837 – 98
    What Child is this, who, laid to rest   719

Doddridge, Philip, 1702 – 51
    O Fount of good, to own thy love (recast by Edward Osler)   777

Ellerton, John, 1826 – 93
    From east to west, from shore to shore (trans.)   709

Fortunatus, Venantius Honorius, 530 – 609
    Sing, my tongue, the glorious battle   728
    The royal banners forward go   729, 730

Fosdick, Harry Emerson, 1878 –
    God of grace and God of glory   778

Franzmann, Martin H., 1907 –
    In Adam we have all been one   759
    O fearful place, where he who knows our heart   774
    O God, O Lord of heaven and earth   758
    O kingly Love, that faithfully   757
    O thou, who hast of thy pure grace   767
    Thy strong word did cleave the darkness   747
    With high delight (trans.)   734

Franzman, Werner H., 1904 –
    Down from the mount of glory   724

Gregory the Great, St., 540 – 604
    Father, we praise thee, now the night is over (ascr.)   788

Harkness, Georgia, 1891 –
    Hope of the world, thou Christ of great compassion   749

Herman, Nikolaus, c. 1480 – 1561
    Let all together praise our God   712

Holmes, John Haynes, 1879 – 1964
    The voice of God is calling   776

Hoppe, Anna Bernadine Dorothy, 1889 – 1941
    O thou, who once in Galilee   751

Janzow, F. Samuel, 1913 –
    From shepherding of stars that gaze   713
    Let all together praise our God (trans.)   712
    We praise, O Christ, your holy name (trans.)   708

Jeffries, Charles
    Speak forth thy word, O Father   760

John of Damascus, St., c. 696 — c. 754
    Come, ye faithful, raise the strain   738
    The day of resurrection   739

Johnson, William, 1906 —
    Deep were his wounds, and red   726

Kempis, Thomas à, 1380 — 1471
    O Love, how deep, how broad, how high   750

Lettermann, Henry L., 1932 —
    Who are these that earnest knock   720

Lindemann, Johann, 1549 — 1631
    In thee is gladness   768

Littledale, Richard Frederick, 1833 — 90
    Come down, O Love divine (paraphr.)   755

Löwenstern, Matthäus Appelles von, 1594 — 1648
    Lord of our life and God of our salvation   786

Lowry, Somerset Corry, 1855 — 1932
    Son of God, eternal Savior   752

Luther, Martin, 1483 — 1546
    Grant peace, we pray, in mercy, Lord (trans. from the antiphon
        Da pacem, Domine)   785
    Lord God, thy praise we sing (trans. from Te Deum)   745
    Now let us pray to God the Holy Ghost   753
    We praise, O Christ, your holy name   708

Milman, Henry Hart, 1791 — 1858
    Ride on, ride on in majesty   727

Monsell, John Samuel Bewley, 1811 — 75
    Sing to the Lord of harvest   793

Moultrie, Gerard, 1829 — 85
    All is o'er, the pain, the sorrow   731
    Let all mortal flesh keep silence (paraphr.)   766

Neale, John Mason, 1818 — 66
    Before the ending of the day (trans.)   790
    Come, ye faithful, raise the strain (trans.)   738
    Creator of the stars of night (trans.)   703
    O sons and daughters of the King (trans.)   735
    O wondrous type! O vision fair (trans.)   723
    Of the Father's love begotten (trans.)   721
    Sing, my tongue, the glorious battle (trans.)   728
    That Easter day with joy was bright (trans.)   737
    The day of resurrection (trans.)   739
    The royal banners forward go (trans.)   729, 730
    With Christ we share a mystic grave   763

Nelson, Horatio Bolton, Earl, 1823 – 1913
From all thy saints in warfare   756

Noel, Caroline Maria, 1817 – 77
At the name of Jesus   743

Oakeley, Frederick, 1802 – 80
O come, all ye faithful (trans.)   710

Osler, Edward, 1798 – 1863
O Fount of good, to own thy love (recast from Philip Doddridge)   777

Patrick, St., c. 372 – 466
I bind unto myself today (ascr.)   746

Pott, Francis, 1832 – 1909
The strife is o'er, the battle done (trans.)   740

Prudentius, Marcus Aurelius Clemens, 348 – c. 413
Of the Father's love begotten   721

Pusey, Philip, 1799 – 1855
Lord of our life and God of our salvation (paraphr.)   786

Rees, Timothy, 1874 – 1939
Holy Spirit, ever dwelling   754

Reid, William Watkins Sr., 1890 –
Forgive us, Lord, for shallow thankfulness   792

Reynolds, William Morton, 1812 – 76
Savior of the nations, come (trans.)   701

Riess, Walter Carl, 1925 –
O Lord of love, whose truth our lives adorn   781

Russell, Arthur Tozer, 1806 – 74
The only Son from heaven (trans.)   722

Sacer, Gottfried Wilhelm, 1635 – 99
See God to heaven ascending   744

Sedulius, Coelius, d. 450
From east to west, from shore to shore   709

Seltz, Martin Luther, 1909 – 67
Christ is arisen (trans.)   741
He whom shepherd men came praising (trans.)   718
In dulci jubilo (trans.)   714
O Savior, rend the heavens wide (trans.)   706
Savior of the nations, come (trans.)   701
See God to heaven ascending (trans.)   744

Smith, Walter Chalmers, 1824 – 1908
Immortal, invisible, God only wise   769

Southwell, Robert, c. 1561–95
    This little Babe so few days old   717

Spannaus, Olive Wise, 1916–
    Lord of all nations, grant me grace   779

Thomas à Kempis, 1380–1471
    O Love, how deep, how broad, how high   750

Tucker, Francis Bland, 1895–
    Our Father, by whose name   782

Tweedy, Henry Hallam, 1868–1953
    Eternal God, whose power upholds   748

Vajda, Jaroslav J., 1919–
    God, my Lord, my Strength, my Place of hiding (paraphr.)   783
    Greet, man, the swiftly changing year (trans.)   791
    Now the silence   770
    Thank the Lord, for he is good   773

Vetter, Georg, 1536–99
    With high delight   734

Wallin, Johan Olof, 1779–1839
    Jehovah, you we glorify   771

Webb, Benjamin, 1820–85
    O Love, how deep, how broad, how high (trans.)   750

Welch, Edward Ashurst, 1860–1932
    We lift our hearts, O Father   780

Werner, Georg, 1589–1643
    Lord Jesus, who, our souls to save (trans. from 14th-century text
      Qui jacuisti mortuus)   732

Wesley, Charles, 1707–88
    Come, thou long-expected Jesus   705
    Lo! He comes with clouds descending   702

Winkworth, Catherine, 1829–78
    In thee is gladness (trans.)   768
    Lord Jesus, who, our souls to save (trans.)   732

Wipo of Burgundy, died c. 1050
    Christians, to the Paschal Victim (ascr.)   741

Woodward, George Ratcliffe, 1848–1934
    This joyful Eastertide   742

Alphabetical Index of Tunes

Ack bliv hos oss (Pax), LM   787

Adeste fideles (Portuguese Hymn), Irregular   710

Agincourt Hymn (Deo gracias), LM   723, 750

Angel's Song (Song 34), LM   775

Ave, virgo virginum (Gaudeamus pariter), 7.6.7.6.D (Trochaic)   738

Beatus vir, LM   779

Bryn Calfaria, 8.7.8.7.4.4.4.7.7   764

Christ ist erstanden, Irregular   741

Christe sanctorum, 11.11.11.5   788

Christum wir sollen loben schon, LM   709

Conditor alme siderum, LM (plainsong)   703

Consolation, CM   707

Cormac, 7.6.7.6.D   776

Cwm Rhondda, 8.7.8.7.4.4.7.7   778

Da pacem (Verleih uns Frieden), 8.7.8.7.8 (plainsong)   785

Das neugeborne Kindelein, 8.8.8.8.8.8   717

Deo gracias (Agincourt Hymn), LM   723, 750

Dies est laetitiae (variant), 7.6.7.6.7.7.5.7.7.6   720

Divinum mysterium, 8.7.8.7.8.7.7   721

Donne secours, 11.10.11.10   749

Down Ampney, 6.6.11.D   755

Ebenezer (Ton-y-Botel), 8.7.8.7.D   747

Erschienen ist der herrlich Tag, LM with alleluia   737

Erstanden ist der heilig Christ, 8.8.8 with alleluias   740

Farley Castle, 10.10.10.10   765

Farrant, CM   763

Forest Green, 8.6.8.6.7.6.8.6   715

Fortunatus New, 8.7.8.7.8.7   728

Freuen wir uns alle, 8.7.8.7   704

Gaudeamus pariter (Ave, virgo virginum), 7.6.7.6.D (Trochaic)   738

Gelobet seist du, Jesu Christ, 8.7.8.8.4   708

Gelobt sei Gott (Vulpius), 8.8.8 with alleluias   736

Gloria (Westminster Carol; Iris) 7.7.7.7 with refrain   711

Greensleeves 8.7.8.7.6.8.6.7   719

He Loves Us Forever, 7.7 with refrain   773

Herr Christ, der einig Gotts Sohn, 7.6.7.6.7.7.6   722

Herr Gott, dich loben wir (Te Deum), Irregular   745

Herzlich tut mich erfreuen, 7.6.7.6.D   739

Ich freu mich, in dem Herren, 7.6.7.6.D 724
In Babilone, 8.7.8.7.D 754
In dir ist Freude, 5.5.7.D.5.5.5.5.5.4.D 768
In dulci jubilo, 6.6.6.6.6.6.5.5 714
Iris (Gloria; Westminster Carol), 7.7.7.7 with refrain 711
Iste confessor, 11.11.11.5 772, 786
Jam lucis, LM (plainsong) 790
Jefferson, 8.7.8.7.D 705
Joanna (St. Denio), 11.11.11.11 769
Kingly Love, LM with refrain 757
King's Banner, The, LM 729
King's Lynn, 7.6.7.6.D 756, 784
King's Majesty, The, LM 727
King's Weston, 6.5.6.5.D 743
Lobt Gott, ihr Christen allzugleich, 8.6.8.6.6 712
Lord, Revive Us, 8.7.8.7.D 752
Love Unknown, 6.6.6.6.4.4.4.4 725
Marlee, 6.6.6.6.8.8 726
Mission, 10.10.10 with alleluias 761, 774
Mit Freuden zart, 8.8.8.8.8.8.8 734
Now, Irregular 770
Nun bitten wir, 10.9.11.9.4 753
Nun komm, der Heiden Heiland, 7.7.7.7 701
Nun lasst uns den Leib begraben, LM 732
Nunc angelorum, Irregular 718
O filii et filiae, 8.8.8 with alleluias 735
O Heiland, reiss die Himmel auf, LM 706
O Seigneur, 6.6.7.6.6.7.D 789
Old 112th (Vater unser), 8.8.8.8.8.8 767
Pán Bůh, 10.4.7.5.6.5 783
Pax (Ack, bliv hos oss), LM 787
Picardy, 8.7.8.7.8.7 702, 766
Pilgrim, CMD 748
Portuguese Hymn (Adeste fideles), Irregular 710
Psalm 146, 8.7.8.7.7.7 731
Quem pastores 8.8.8.7 (Trochaic) 718
Resonet in laudibus (refrain only), 11.11 718
Rhosymedre, 6.6.6.6.8.8.8 782
Rok nový, 8.8.8.6 791
St. Denio (Joanna), 11.11.11.11 769
St. Patrick's Breastplate, LMD 746
Saints' Delight, The, CM 759
Salem, CM 751
Shepherding, 8.6.8.6.6 713
Song 20, SM 762
Song 34 (Angel's Song), LM 775

Song 67, CM 777
Sonne der Gerechtigkeit, 7.7.7.7.4 733
Speak Forth Thy Word, 7.6.7.6.D 760
Sursum corda, 10.10.10.10 781, 792
Te Deum (Herr Gott, dich loben wir). Irregular 745
Tempus adest floridum, 7.6.7.6.D 716
Ter Sanctus, 8.8.4.6.10 771
Ton-y-Botel (Ebenezer), 8.7.8.7.D 747
Vater unser (Old 112th), 8.8.8.8.8.8 767
Verleih uns Frieden (Da pacem), 8.7.8.7.8 (plainsong) 785
Vexilla regis, LM (plainsong) 730
Victimae paschali, Irregular (plainsong) 741
Vruechten, 6.7.6.7 with refrain 742
Vulpius (Gelobt sei Gott), 8.8.8 with alleluias 736
We Lift Our Hearts, 7.6.7.6 780
Westminster Carol (Gloria; Iris), 7.7.7.7 with refrain 711
Wie lieblich ist der Maien, 7.6.7.6.D 793
Wittenberg New, LMD 758
Zeuch ein zu deinen Toren, 7.6.7.6.6.7.7.6 744

Index of First Lines and Titles

All is o'er, the pain, the sorrow	731
Angels we have heard on high	711
At the Lamb's high feast we sing	733
At the name of Jesus	743
Before the ending of the day	790
Christ is arisen	741
Christians, to the Paschal Victim	741
Come down, O Love divine	755
Come, thou long-expected Jesus	705
Come, ye faithful, raise the strain	738
Creator of the stars of night	703
Deep were his wounds, and red	726
Down from the mount of glory	724
Eternal God, whose power upholds	748
Father, we praise thee, now the night is over	788
Forgive us, Lord, for shallow thankfulness	792
From all thy saints in warfare	756
From east to west, from shore to shore	709
From shepherding of stars that gaze	713
Gentle Mary laid her Child	716
Go labor on; spend and be spent	775
God, my Lord, my Strength, my Place of hiding	783
God of grace and God of glory	778
God's own Son is born a child	718
Good Christian men, rejoice and sing	736
Grant peace, we pray, in mercy, Lord	785
Greet, man, the swiftly changing year	791
Hark! A thrilling voice is sounding	704
He whom shepherd men came praising	718
Here, O my Lord, I see thee face to face	765
Holy Spirit, ever dwelling	754
Hope of the world, thou Christ of great compassion	749
I bind unto myself today	746
Immortal, invisible, God only wise	769
In Adam we have all been one	759
In dulci jubilo	714

In thee is gladness   768
Jehovah, you we glorify   771
Let all mortal flesh keep silence   766
Let all together praise our God   712
Lo! He comes with clouds descending   702
Lord, enthroned in heavenly splendor   764
Lord God, thy praise we sing   745
Lord Jesus, who, our souls to save   732
Lord of all nations, grant me grace   779
Lord of our life and God of our salvation   786
My song is love unknown   725
Now let us pray to God the Holy Ghost   753
Now the silence   770
O come, all ye faithful, joyful and triumphant   710
O fearful place, where he who knows our heart   774
O Fount of good, to own thy love   777
O God, O Lord of heaven and earth   758
O God of earth and altar   784
O God of love, O King of peace   787
O kingly Love, that faithfully   757
O little town of Bethlehem   715
O Lord of love, whose truth our lives adorn   781
O Love, how deep, how broad, how high   750
O Savior, rend the heavens wide   706
O sons and daughters of the King   735
O thou, who hast of thy pure grace   767
O thou, who once in Galilee   751
O wondrous type! O vision fair   723
Of the Father's love begotten   721
Only-begotten, Word of God eternal   772
Our Father, by whose name   782
Quempas Celebration   718
Ride on, ride on in majesty!   727
Savior of the nations, come   701
See God to heaven ascending   744
Sing, my tongue, the glorious battle   728
Sing to the Lord of harvest   793
Son of God, eternal Savior   752
Speak forth thy Word, O Father   760
Stand, soldier of the cross   762
Te Deum, Luther's   745
Thank the Lord, for he is good   773
That Easter day with joy was bright   737

The day of resurrection | 739
The glorious angels came today | 718
The King shall come when morning dawns | 707
The only Son from heaven | 722
The royal banners forward go | 729, 730
The sending, Lord, springs from thy yearning heart | 761
The strife is o'er, the battle done | 740
The voice of God is calling | 776
This joyful Eastertide | 742
This little Babe so few days old | 717
Thy strong arm did cleave the darkness | 747
Vexilla Regis Celebration | 729, 730
Victimae Paschali Celebration | 741
We lift our hearts, O Father | 780
We praise, O Christ, your holy name | 708
What Child is this, who, laid to rest | 719
When morning gilds the skies | 789
Who are these that earnest knock | 720
With Christ we share a mystic grave | 763
With high delight let us unite | 734